US Carrier Aircraft of World War 2

When the US was catapulted into World War 2 by the Japanese attack on Pearl Harbor, the American war machine was still in low gear. The US Navy in particular was operating a fleet of old-fashioned and outmoded aircraft that were no match for the battles to come. The US aviation industry on the other hand had been playing a key role in supplying orders to the hard-pressed European allied forces, so when the call to battle came, expansion was on an astonishing scale. With access to practically unlimited resources, advances in aircraft technology were rapid and the re-equipment programme of the US Navy became a decisive factor in the fight against Japan.

During early operations in the Pacific, the US Navy's fighter squadrons relied almost exclusively upon the Grumman Wildcat, an aircraft that was vulnerable against the superior Japanese Zero. Fewer than 250 were actually in service in December 1941, but nearly 8,000 were eventually built before it gave way to the legendary Hellcat and Corsair. It was on the latter two types that the US Navy built its success in repelling Japanese attacks on its ships and shore bases throughout the Pacific area, eventually achieving complete air supremacy.

Meanwhile, a new generation of torpedo and dive bombers were also playing a critical role in carrier operations where battles were won or lost at sea, by individual as well as collective exploits. Slow in flight, many-a-torpedo bomber depended upon the protection brought about by its own carrier-based escort fighters. Their bombing runs were usually the most critical time for the crew and their torpedo-laden machines, when their plodding nature and projected attack runs made them easy targets. Aircraft names like the Dauntless and Avenger became synonymous with heroic acts of tragedy as well as triumph.

The pace of development and production of US Navy aviation was relentless, though sheer quantity of output was not always matched by technical quality. A number of types failed to make it past the prototype testing stage and achieve production, while other more revolutionary types, such as the US Navy's first jets, entered production too late to see active service.

During World War 2, the US Navy went from operating ageing biplane fighters, to flying some of the most powerful aircraft the World had ever seen. This is that story… **Allan Burney**

AVIATION ARCHIVE SERIES

This issue of 'Aviation Archive' represents a pictorial tribute to the aircraft and pilots that fought for the US Navy during World War 2. The aircraft types are listed in chronological sequence of maiden flights, which provides a graphic insight into the technological advances over the period 1941-44. As ever, the photographs have been carefully selected out of the extensive 'Aeroplane Archive' for their historic and rarity value, supplemented by other sources. The images are complemented by 'period' cutaways from the talented pens of the 'Flight' and 'Aeroplane' artists of the era and by contemporary profiles by Andy Hay and Rolando Ugolini. We are also greatly indebted to authors Bruce Hales-Dutton and Warren Thompson and the aviation artist Mark Postlethwaite.

Aviation Archive Series

US Carrier Aircraft of World War 2

- **Editor:** Allan Burney • **Design:** Key Studio
- **Publisher and Managing Director:** Adrian Cox • **Executive Chairman:** Richard Cox • **Commercial Director:** Ann Saundry • **Distribution:** Seymour Distribution Ltd +44 (0)20 7429 4000
- **Printing:** Warners (Midlands) PLC, The Maltings, Manor Lane, Bourne, Lincs PE10 9PH.

US Carrier Aircraft of World War 2

Grumman F3F

Although still in service at the beginning of World War 2, the barrel-chested Grumman F3F fighter was not used in anger as it was withdrawn from front-line operations prior to the Japanese attack on Pearl Harbor. Nevertheless, it retains a certain iconic appeal, not least because it was the US Navy's ultimate biplane and as such marked the end of one era and the beginning of another. Indeed, perhaps the F3F's greatest claim to fame was that it was the direct ancestor of the legendary F4F Wildcat.

The Grumman F3F came about as an improved form of the preceding F2F biplane fighter. The US Navy's experience with the F2F revealed issues with stability and unfavourable spin characteristics, prompting the 15 October 1934 contract for the improved XF3F-1, placed before F2F deliveries began. The contract also required a capability for ground attack, in addition to the design's fighter role. Powered by the same Pratt & Whitney R-1535-72 Twin Wasp Junior engine as the F2F, the fuselage was lengthened and wing area increased over the earlier design. A reduction in wheel diameter allowed greater fuselage streamlining, eliminating the prominent bulge behind the cowling of the F2F. However, the similar biplane wing arrangement remained. The prototype, BuNo 9727, was delivered and

first flown on 20 March 1935 with company test pilot Jimmy Collins making three flights that day. The new design was extensively tested for dive recovery, but during trials the aircraft broke up in mid-air, crashing on a cemetery and killing Collins.

A second strengthened prototype was built, but it also crashed following the pilot's bailout during an unsuccessful spin recovery. The airframe was salvaged and rebuilt to fly again during June of 1935. An order for 54 F3F-1 fighters was placed on 24 August of that year, following the conclusion of the flight test programme. The first production F3F-1 was delivered on 29 January 1936 to the test group at NAS Anacostia, with squadron service beginning in March to VF-5B of the USS *Ranger* and VF-6B of the USS *Saratoga*. Marine squadron VF-4M received the last six in January 1937.

Wanting to take advantage of the powerful new 950hp Wright R-1820 supercharged radial engine, Grumman began work on the F3F-2

without a contract; the order for 81 aircraft was not placed until 25 July 1936, two days before the type's first flight. The engine's larger diameter changed the cowling's appearance, making the aircraft look even more rotund, though top speed increased to 255mph (410km/h) at 12,000ft (3,658m). The entire F3F-2 production series was delivered between 1937 and 1938.

The final production model was the F3F-3, which was fitted with various propellers, split landing-flaps, modified cowling, and other devices intended to improve overall performance. Twenty-seven F3F-3s were delivered in 1938-39, which brought the overall production of F3F series aircraft to 164 aircraft. Most of the F3F-3s served with VF-5 (USS *Yorktown*) or VF-7 (USS *Wasp*). By 1939, all US Navy and Marines Corps fighter squadrons were equipped with F2F or F3F series aircraft. But, in truth the stubby biplane was already outmoded by the time it entered service, a fact compounded by its poor cockpit visibility, light armament and lack of suitability as a weapons platform because of longitudinal instability. By 1941 the type was withdrawn from frontline service and relegated to training duties and retired completely two years later. Nevertheless, as the last biplane fighter in the US inventory, the F3F had earned itself an affectionate place in aviation history.

Below: It is difficult to believe that when World War 2 broke out, the stubby Grumman F3F was the US Navy's premier front-line fighter. However, by the time the US entered the conflict, the obsolete biplane had been withdrawn from front-line service and was thus destined never to see combat. This aircraft hails from VF-4 in the late 1930s.

Grumman F3F

Crew:	One
Length:	23ft 2in (7.06m)
Wingspan:	32ft (9.75m)
Height:	9ft 4in (2.84m)
Empty weight:	3,285lb (1,490kg)
Loaded weight:	4,795lb (2,175kg)
Powerplant:	Wright R-1820-22 Cyclone 9-cylinder radial engine of 950hp (710kW)
Top speed:	264mph at 15,250ft
Service ceiling:	33,200ft (10,120m)
Armament:	1× 0.30 in (7.62mm) M1919 machine gun, 500 rounds (left), 1× 0.50 in (12.7mm) M2 machine gun, 200 rounds (right)
Ordnance:	2× 116lb (52.6kg) Mk IV bombs, one located under each wing

Left: The first production Grumman F3F-1 was delivered to the test group at NAS Anacostia on 29 January 1936. Although the F3F was the product of another age, it played an important part in the evolution of US Navy fighters and gave birth to the legendary Wildcat.

Below left: The first production Grumman F3F-2 (BuNo 0967) undergoing a gear retraction check inside the NACA hangar at Langley. It was easier to suspend the aircraft from the hangar ceiling to perform this check than to jack it up.

Below: The Grumman F3F-2 production line, with aircraft in various states of construction. The design was quickly superseded by monoplane fighters and in the event only 164 were built.

Left: **Three Grumman F3F-3 fighters used for flight training at NAS Corpus Christi in 1942. The final version, the F3F-3, came about because of delays in the development of the F4F. It incorporated a smaller diameter propeller, a modified cowling and a cockpit canopy similar to that used on the F4F. Only 27 of this version were ordered with the first aircraft being assigned to the carrier USS Yorktown (CV-5).**

Below left: **Visibility out of the F3F cockpit was not good, especially when taxying and during final approach. Nevertheless, the aircraft was popular with its pilots when it first entered service, though its limitations quickly became apparent. The chevron on top of the wing was a visual device to aid formation flying.**

Right: **This impressive formation shot represents a tenth of all F3Fs built and clearly shows the variety and complexity of colour schemes worn by the individual aircraft.**

Below: **A US Navy Landing Signal Officer guides Grumman F3Fs during pilot training at NAS Corpus Christi, Texas.**

Below right: **A pilot pre-flights his aircraft. The F3Fs were colourful beasts. Sporting numerous bands, chevrons, cowlings and panels of red, blue, green, white and yellow, the colours were the US Navy's 1930s code to denote squadron, carrier affiliation, pilot rank, even an aircraft's appointed flying position in its section.**

Curtiss SBC Helldiver

Somewhat ironically, the last military biplane procured by the US Navy began life as a monoplane. The Curtiss SBC Helldiver was a two-seat scout/dive-bomber delivered in 1937, but which became obsolete even before World War 2 started and was kept well away from combat with Axis fighters. However, it crossed over two eras of aviation, its biplane design being countered by a fuselage encased with metalwork and of streamlined shape.

Requiring a new two-seat carrier-based fighter, in 1932 the US Navy gave the Curtiss-Wright Corporation a contract to design a parasol two-seat monoplane with retractable undercarriage. The US Navy designated the prototype as XF12C-1. The Model 73 was powered by a single Wright R-1510-92 Whirlwind 14 series radial piston engine and achieved first flight in 1933, though by the end of the year the US Navy had revamped its requirement and categorised the prototype as the XS4C-1 scout plane. Following yet

another change of heart, its role became that of a scout-bomber in January 1934 and a Wright R-1820 Cyclone engine was installed. Extensive trials followed and during a dive test in September 1934 there was structural failure of the wing and the XSBC-1, as it had become designated, was extensively damaged, though its pilot survived. The parasol wing was clearly unsuitable for the dive-bombing requirement and a new prototype was ordered as the XSBC-2 (Model 77), this having biplane wings and a Wright R-1510-12 Whirlwind 14 engine. Finally, in March 1936, this engine was replaced by a

Pratt & Whitney R-1535-82 Twin Wasp Junior engine, and the designation changed yet again to XSBC-3. The production SBC-3 (Model 77A), of which the US Navy ordered 83 on 29 August 1936, was generally similar and first deliveries, to US Navy Squadron VS-5, were made on 17 July 1937 with the first batch of carrier-based aircraft going to the USS Yorktown.

By all reports, the SBC Helldiver was an easy aircraft to fly and handled well in its dive-bombing role. The crew of two sat in tandem under a long- glazed canopy with heavy framing with generally poor forward visibility especially during take-off and landing.

The SBC Helldiver could achieve a top speed of 234mph, but its service ceiling was limited to 24,000ft.

Armament was poor and included a pair of 0.30 calibre machine guns (one forward fixed for the pilot and the other on a trainable mount in the rear cockpit) with an optional 1,000lb bombload along the fuselage centreline.

Inevitably, advances in aviation technology rapidly overtook the SBC Helldiver. When the Japanese Empire unleashed its surprise attack on the US Naval base at Pearl Harbor, Hawaii, on 7 December 1941, thus catapulting the US into World War 2, the SBC was already obsolete. Regardless, the biplane dive-bomber soldiered on for a time longer with both US Navy and Marine Corps branches aboard such active carriers as the USS Hornet before being relegated to hack duties and service as an advanced trainer for units in Florida. The last aircraft was struck from the US Navy roster in October 1944.

Meanwhile, foreign interest for the concept of a dive-bomber had led to orders for 50 SBC-4s for the French Navy. Like other military equipment earmarked for use by France from the US, this delivery would arrive too late to be of much use, though five were diverted to the RAF which named them the Curtiss Cleveland Mk I and used them for training.

Although the SBC Helldiver was not destined to have a long US service career, it did however make a lasting contribution by serving as the key platform in developing dive bombing tactics and honing aircrew skills crucial to winning the war in the Pacific. Not a bad legacy for the US Navy's last biplane aircraft.

A US Navy Curtiss SBC-4 Helldiver (BuNo 1813) assigned to Naval Air Reserve Air Base New York, Floyd Bennett Field (note the NRAB New York insignia on the fuselage). This SBC-4 was one of the aircraft transferred to USAAC on 8 June 1940 and then to the French Navy. Forty four were loaded aboard the French aircraft carrier Béarn at Dartmouth, Nova Scotia. France surrendered while Béarn was crossing the Atlantic and the ship turned south to Martinique, where the SBC-4s corroded in the humid Caribbean climate while waiting on a hillside near Fort-de-France. Five aircraft left in Canada were used by the RAF as instructional airframes.

Left: A US Navy Helldiver making a simulated carrier approach during land-based training in preparation for operations at sea. The Helldiver design was characterised by its staggered, uneven span biplane wing arrangement with thick outboard struts, cabling and skeletal inboard struts designed to hold the wings in place during dive-bombing operations.

Right: A formation of three SBC-4 Helldivers assigned to Naval Air Reserve Air Base New York, Floyd Bennett Field. Note the NRAB New York insignia on the fuselages of the aircraft.

Below: An SBC-3 Helldiver (BuNo 0543) of Scouting Squadron Five (VS-5). The squadron was assigned to the aircraft carrier USS Yorktown (CV-5) and flew the aircraft from 1937 to 1940. This particular aircraft was retired on 6 July 1943.

Above: A chilly scene at Naval Air Reserve Air Base Minneapolis as Curtiss SBC-4 Helldiver (BuNo 1831) starts up. Reserve Scouting Squadron Ten (VS-10R) and Marine Reserve Scouting Squadron Six (VMS-6R) operated SBC-4s at the base. Note the Naval Air Reserve insignia on the aircraft's cowling.

Below: A Helldiver pilot completes his pre-flight checks before taxying out in SBC-3 (BuNo 0512) of VS-3. Normally assigned to USS Saratoga (CV-3), VS-3 flew SBC-3s during the period 1938-1940.

Curtiss SBC Helldiver

Crew:	Two, pilot and gunner
Length:	28ft 2in (8.57m)
Wingspan:	34ft (10.36m)
Height:	10ft 5in (3.17m)
Empty weight:	4,552lb (2,065kg)
Loaded weight:	7,080lb (3,211kg)
Powerplant:	Wright R-1820-34 radial engine of 850hp
Top speed:	234mph at 15,200ft
Service ceiling:	24,000ft (7,320m)
Armament:	1× 0.30in (7.62mm) forward-firing M1919 Browning machine gun, 1× 0.30in (7.62 mm) flexible rearward-firing machine gun
Ordnance:	1× bomb of up to 1,000lb (454 kg)

Above: A US Navy Curtiss SBC-3 Helldiver (BuNo 0571) assigned to Scouting Squadron Three (VS-3) pictured in flight near San Diego, CA; the side number '3-S-1' indicates that this is the commander's aircraft. Normally assigned to USS Saratoga (CV-3), VS-3 flew SBC-3s during 1938-1940. This SBC-3 ended its life as a ground instructional airframe at NAS Jacksonville, FL, and was scrapped on 31 May 1943.

Below: In its natural environment, this Helldiver of Scouting Squadron VS-6 from the aircraft carrier USS Enterprise (CV-6), flies low past the Sims-class destroyer USS Mustin (DD-413), during exercises on 26 May 1940.

Douglas TBD Devastator

Sadly, the Douglas TBD Devastator torpedo bomber will forever be remembered for its tragic involvement during the Battle of Midway and the sacrifice of its crews. Although the aircraft was immediately removed from front-line operations, it should not be forgotten that just five years earlier it was deemed to be the most advanced aircraft of its kind anywhere in the World. As such, it was the US Navy's first all-metal mount and the first to feature hydraulically-assisted folding wings (for improved carrier storage). It also had the distinction of being first US Navy monoplane to be fielded in quantity on its carriers.

The Douglas TBD Devastator was born out of a US Navy requirement issued in 1934 for a carrier-based torpedo bomber. The Douglas entry was one of the winners of the competition, which also saw orders placed for the Northrop BT-1 (which would evolve into the SBD Dauntless), the Brewster SBA and the Vought SB2U Vindicator.

The Devastator emerged in prototype form as the XTBD-1 to which first flight was recorded on 15 April 1935. Only a single prototype would ever be constructed and evaluated, this being powered by a single Pratt & Whitney XR-1830-60 radial piston engine. The XTBD-1 was accepted into service with the US Navy as the TBD-1 and these entered production with a Pratt & Whitney R-1830-64 series Twin Wasp radial piston engine of 850hp.

The Devastator marked a large number of 'firsts' for the US Navy. It was the first widely used carrier-based monoplane as well as the first all-metal naval aircraft, the first with a totally enclosed cockpit, the first with power-actuated (hydraulically) folding wings and

A US Navy Douglas TBD-1 Devastator (BuNo 0331) of Torpedo Squadron Five (VT-5) pictured circa 1938-1940. Note the squadron insignia and 'Navy E' on the fuselage beneath the cockpit. In addition, this view of the aircraft reveals the wing chevrons carried on naval aircraft during this period.

in these respects the TBD was revolutionary. A semi-retractable landing gear was fitted, with the wheels designed to protrude 10in (250mm) below the wings to permit a 'wheels-up' landing which might limit damage to the aircraft. A crew of three was normally carried beneath a large 'greenhouse' canopy almost half the length of the aircraft. The pilot sat in front; a rear gunner/radio operator took the rearmost position, while the bombardier occupied the middle seat. During a bombing run, the bombardier lay prone, sliding into position under the

Above: **The Douglas XTBD-1 pictured in Virginia skies. This particular aircraft made its maiden flight on 15 April 1935 and underwent performance trials at NAS Anacostia, NAS Norfolk, and NPG Dahlgren until November 1935. After completing carrier trials on board USS** Lexington **(CV-2) off the coast of California, the aircraft returned to the Douglas plant in 1936 for overhaul and minor modifications, including a redesigned canopy. Returned to the US Navy in December 1936, it was employed in flight testing until scrapped on 10 September 1943.**

Douglas TBD Devastator

Crew:	Three; pilot, torpedo officer/navigator, radioman/gunner
Length:	35ft (10.67m)
Wingspan:	50ft (15.24m)
Height:	15ft 1in (4.6m)
Empty weight:	5,600lb (2,540kg)
Loaded weight:	9,289lb (4,213kg)
Powerplant:	Pratt & Whitney R-1830-64 Twin Wasp radial of 900hp
Top speed:	206mph at 8,000ft
Service ceiling:	19,500ft (5,945m)
Armament:	1× forward-firing 0.30in (7.62mm) or 0.50in (12.7mm) machine gun, 1× 0.30in (7.62mm) machine gun in rear cockpit (later increased to two)
Ordnance:	1× Mark 13 torpedo or 1× 1,000lb (454kg) bomb or 2× 500lb (227kg) bombs or 12× 100lb (45kg) bombs

pilot to sight through a window in the bottom of the fuselage, using the Norden Bombsight. Maximum speed was listed at 206mph with a range of 435 miles and a service ceiling of 19,700ft.

In terms of defensive armament, the TBD Devastator was limited. The pilot controlled a single forward-firing 7.62mm general purpose machine gun or 12.7mm heavy machine gun to engage targets ahead of his position, suitable for strafing actions during the bombing run. The rear gunner operated a single 7.62mm machine gun, though this was later upgraded

to include a pair of 7.62mm machine guns for slightly improved defence. However, it was in its offensive prowess that a torpedo bomber would ultimately succeed or fail. As such, primary armament for the TBD Devastator family was a single 1,200lb Mark 13 torpedo for attacking ships along their broadsides.

A total of 129 of the type were purchased by the US Navy's Bureau of Aeronautics (BuAer), and starting from 1937 began to equip the carriers USS *Saratoga*, *Enterprise*, *Lexington*, *Wasp*, *Hornet*, *Yorktown* and *Ranger*. In pre-war use, TBD units were engaged in training and other operational activities, but the US Navy was already aware that the TBD had become outclassed by fighters and bombers of other nations. Although a replacement was in the works, when the US entered World War 2 the Devastator was still in front-line service with over 100 operational.

With the Japanese attack on Pearl Harbor, the Devastator began to see combat action. Taking part in attacks on Japanese shipping in the Gilbert Islands in February 1942, TBDs from USS *Enterprise* had little success. This was largely due to problems associated with the Mark 13 torpedo. A delicate weapon, the Mark 13 required the pilot to drop it from no higher than 120ft and no faster than 150mph making the aircraft extremely vulnerable during its attack. Once dropped, the Mark 13 had issues with running too deep or simply failing to

explode on impact. For torpedo attacks, the bombardier was typically left on the carrier and the Devastator flew with a crew of two. Additional raids that spring saw TBDs attack Wake and Marcus Islands, as well as targets off New Guinea with mixed results. The highlight of the Devastator's career came during the Battle of the Coral Sea when the type aided in sinking the light carrier *Shoho*. Subsequent attacks against the larger Japanese carriers the next day proved fruitless.

At Midway, a total of 41 Devastators, the majority of the type still operational, were launched from *Hornet*, *Enterprise* and *Yorktown* to attack the Japanese fleet. The Devastator proved to be a death trap for its crews. It lacked manoeuvrability, had light defensive weaponry and poor armour relative to the weapons of the time. Moreover, its speed on a glide-bombing approach was a mere 200mph (320km/h), making it easy prey for fighters and defensive guns alike. Tragically, during the battle, only four TBDs made it back to *Enterprise*, none to *Hornet* and two to *Yorktown*, without scoring a torpedo hit. This brought the aircraft's combat career to an inglorious end.

In the wake of Midway, the US Navy withdrew its remaining TBDs and squadrons transitioned to the newly arriving Avenger. The 39 TBDs remaining in the inventory were assigned to training roles and by 1944 the type was no longer in the US Navy's inventory.

*Above: **Three US Navy TBD-1 Devastators of VT-2 pictured in formation. Note the squadron insignia, a 'bombman' astride a torpedo, on the fuselage beneath the cockpit. The three TBDs had much different careers: TBD-1, BuNo 0292, was delivered to VT-2 as 2-T-9. The aircaft was lost on 12 January 1940 with VT-3 in a mid-air collision. The crew bailed out safely. TBD-1, BuNo 0292, was delivered to VT-2 as 2-T-7, but was later lost with VT-5 (as 5-T-7) when it crash-landed in the Jaluit Atoll lagoon, Marshall Islands, on 1 February 1942. The crew became prisoners of war. TBD-1, BuNo 0293, 2-T-8 was lost with VT-8 during the Battle of Midway on 4 June 1942.***

*Above right: **Left side view of the pilot's cockpit of a Douglas TBD-1 torpedo bomber, 20 August 1937. At that point, the Devastator was the most advanced aircraft flying for the US Navy, however by the time of the Japanese attack on Pearl Harbor the TBD was already outdated.***

*Right: **Douglas TBD-1 torpedo bombers pictured in various stages of assembly at Douglas Aircraft Company's Santa Monica, CA, plant. Note that the aircraft already carry the markings of Torpedo Squadron 2 (VT-2), which received its first delivery of Devastators in 1938.***

Above: **A US Navy Douglas TBD-1 (BuNo 0325, 6-T-4) of VT-6 from the aircraft carrier USS Enterprise (CV-6) making a practice drop with a Mark 13 torpedo on 20 October 1941. TBD-1 0325 was destined to be the last surviving Devastator, being stricken on 30 November 1944 and subsequently scrapped.**

Left: **Three Devastators assigned to the Naval Operational Training Command at Naval Air Station Miami, in flight over South Florida, 1942/43. NAS Miami and NAS Ft Lauderdale were home to Operational Training Units for the instruction of US Navy torpedo-bomber pilots.**

Below: **With wings folded, TBD-1 Devastators of VT-4 cram the deck of the aircraft carrier USS Ranger (CV-4) in 1942. This photograph was taken while the ship was at anchor in Cuba. Established in 1941, VT-4 operated TBD-1s from Ranger until the autumn of 1942.**

Left: During the Battle of Midway, TBD-1s of VT-6 are prepared for launch from USS Enterprise (CV-6) at about 07.30-07.40hrs, 4 June 1942. Eleven of the 14 TBDs operated from Enterprise on that fateful day are visible. Three more TBDs and ten F4F fighters must still be pushed into position before launching can begin. The TBD in the left front is Number Two (BuNo 1512), flown by Ensign Severin L. Rombach and Aviation Radioman 2nd Class W.F. Glenn. Along with eight other VT-6 aircraft, this plane and its crew were lost attacking Japanese aircraft carriers just two hours later.

Overall: A painting depicting a Devastator making a torpedo attack against a Japanese aircraft carrier at the Battle of Midway, 4 June 1942. Forty-one Devastators were involved in the action but they encountered heavy losses due to their slow speed, poor manoeuvrability, lack of planned air cover and misplaced assault. Not a single direct hit was recorded from all of the torpedoes launched in the attacks and only six aircraft returned home. The sacrifice, however, was not in vain as the attack forced the Japanese to undertake unplanned actions and expose weaknesses in their invasion flotilla. At least one Japanese heavy cruiser was eventually lost at the hands of the Devastators.

The aircraft carrier USS Yorktown (CV-5) operating in the Pacific in February 1942, photographed from a Douglas TBD-1 that has just taken off from her deck. Other TBD and SBD aircraft are also ready to be launched, while an F4F-3 Wildcat fighter is parked on the outrigger just forward of the island. The other ships in company include the fleet oiler USS Guadaloupe (AO-32), a destroyer and a heavy cruiser. This view has been retouched to censor the CXAM-radar antenna mounted atop Yorktown's foremast.

Above: **The Japanese light aircraft carrier Shokaku attacked by USS Yorktown (CV-5) aircraft during the Battle of Coral Sea, on the morning of 8 May 1942. Flames from a bomb hit on her forecastle are visible, as are smoke and splashes from dive bombers' near misses off her starboard side. Photographed from a TBD-1 Devastator of VT-5, what appear to be erratic torpedo tracks are visible in the lower left (inset) and note the Douglas TBD Devastator in lower centre/left and two or three other US Navy aircraft visible above the burning carrier (above).**

Right: **A Devastator of VT-6 just prior to trapping on board the aircraft carrier USS Enterprise (CV-6) in 1942.**

Vought SB2U Vindicator

The Vought SB2U Vindicator carrier-based dive-bomber combined old-fashioned biplane technology and structure with a monoplane layout. Obsolete at the outbreak of World War 2, it was underpowered and vulnerable. Although Vindicators still remained in service at the time of the Battle of Midway, all had been withdrawn to training units by 1943.

The Vindicator was born through a 1934 US Navy requirement calling for a new carrier-based bomb delivery platform in either monoplane or biplane form. The US Navy received proposals from six manufacturers and Vought submitted designs in both categories, the XSB2U-1 and XSB3U-1 respectively. Inevitably, the monoplane proved superior and production started on 26 October 1936. There proved several major marks of the Vindicator line beginning with the XSB2U-1. Only a single prototype was completed before the SB2U-1 production model arrived, this powered by the R-1535-86 engine of 825hp. Fifty-four of the type were produced. Then came the SB2U-2, which was more or less a slightly revised form (primarily in equipment) of the SB2U-1, and 58 were added.

The Vindicator, as it had now become known, was of conventional low-wing monoplane configuration with a retractable main landing gear, the pilot and tail gunner being seated in tandem under a long greenhouse-style canopy. The fuselage was of steel tube construction, covered with aluminum panels from the nose to the rear cockpit with a fabric-covered rear fuselage, while the folding cantilever wing was of all-metal construction. Its Pratt & Whitney R-1535 Twin-Wasp Junior radial engine drove a two-blade constant-speed propeller, which was intended to act as a dive brake during a dive bombing attack. In the event, this was never employed and instead the SB2U dived with its landing gear extended, using a lesser dive angle. A single 1,000lb (450kg) bomb could

Left: Flight deck operations aboard the US Navy aircraft carrier USS Ranger (CV-4) on 19 November 1941, showing Vought SB2U-3 Vindicators of Scouting Squadron 41 (VS-41) and VS-42 getting ready for a patrol flight, and a Grumman F4F-3 Wildcat of VF-41. Note the marking schemes in use on the aircraft, the white codes, and the crew of the machine in the foreground in cold weather gear.

be carried on a swinging trapeze to allow it to clear the propeller in a steep dive, while further bombs could be carried under the wings to give a maximum bombload of 1,500lb (680kg). SB2U armament consisted of a flexible rear-firing machine gun and one fixed firing-forward machine gun.

The Vindicator entered service in 1937 but was already obsolete by 1940, partly because the additional weight of combat equipment had very adverse effects on its already marginal performance. Nevertheless, a British version of the SB2U Vindicator was exported for use by the Fleet Air Arm of the Royal Navy where it was called the Chesapeake.

Of the SB2Us in US Navy service about 30% were lost in combat while about 50% were casualties associated with accidents during operational training and carrier deck landing. They were among the many aircraft destroyed during the Japanese attack on Pearl Harbor while other Vindicators were with the Atlantic fleet on the aircraft carriers USS *Ranger*, USS *Wasp*, and the USS *Yorktown*, involved with anti-submarine patrol, and training activities. Air Group Nine, destined for *Essex*, trained in Vindicators aboard the escort carrier *Charger*, but they transitioned to the Douglas

*Below: **The first production Vought SB2U-1 Vindicator (BuNo 0726) being tested in the 30 x 60ft full-scale wind tunnel at the National Advisory Committee for Aeronautics (NACA), Langley Research Center, at Hampton, VA, on 24 September 1937.***

SBD Dauntless before *Essex* joined the war. Meanwhile, VMSB-131 and VMSB-241 were the only two USMC squadrons that fielded the Marine-specific SB2U-3 between March 1941 and September 1943. The desperate attempt to keep Midway Island secure from Japanese invasion brought the SB2U Vindicators of VMSB-241 into combat, with the type suffering heavy losses. During one attack, Capt Richard E. Fleming, piloting an SB2U Vindicator, led a dive-bombing assault on the Japanese battlecruiser *Mogami*. For his heroic efforts, he was posthumously awarded a Medal of Honor.

By the end of 1942, US Fleet SB2Us had been replaced by the Douglas SBD Dauntless dive bomber.

Vought SB2U Vindicator

Crew:	Two, pilot and gunner
Length:	34ft (10.36m)
Wingspan:	42ft (12.8m)
Height:	10ft 3in (3.12m)
Empty weight:	4,713lb (2,138kg)
Loaded weight:	6,379lb (2,893kg)
Powerplant:	Pratt & Whitney R-1535-96 Twin Wasp Jr radial engine of 825hp
Top speed:	251mph
Service ceiling:	27,500ft (8,382m)
Armament:	1× forward firing 0.30in (7.62mm) M1919 Browning machine gun in starboard wing, 1× 0.30in (7.62mm) machine gun in flexible mount for the tail gunner
Ordnance:	1× 1,000lb (454kg) or 500lb (227kg) bomb

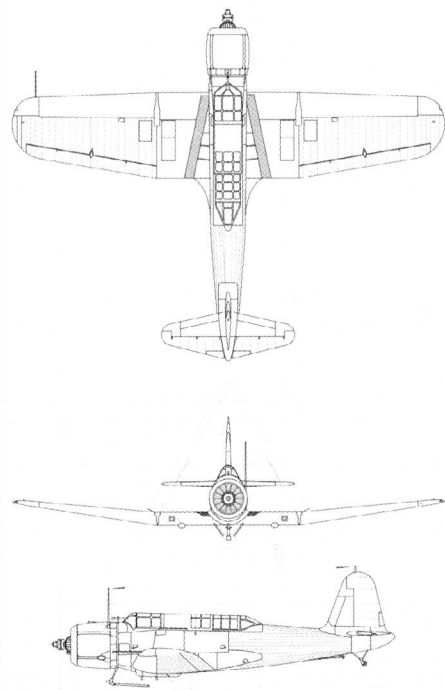

*Top left: **A US Marine Corps Vought SB2U-3 Vindicator of Marine Scouting Squadron VMS-1 circa 1940. Airmen with experience in more modern aircraft spoke disparagingly of SB2Us as 'vibrators' or 'wind indicators' in their latter combat assignments.***

*Above left: **A US Navy Vought SB2U-1 Vindicator dive-bomber assigned to Bombing Squadron 3 (VB-3) aboard the aircraft carrier USS Saratoga (CV-3). VB-3 was the first squadron to be equipped with the SB2U in 1937.***

*Left: **The US Navy aircraft carrier USS Ranger (CV-4) at sea on 10 November 1939. The aircraft on deck are mainly Vought SB2U Vindicators.***

U.S.S. WASP
DECK EDGE ELEVATOR
IS AFT & DOWN FROM AFT END OF
GUN PLATFORM.
WING ELEVATOR BETWEEN DECKS
QUINCY, MASS.   JUNE 1940.

*Left: **Vought SB2U-2 Vindicator (BuNo 1376) from VS-72 pictured on the deck edge elevator of the aircraft carrier USS Wasp (CV-7) at Quincy, MA, in June 1940. The elevator consisted of a platform for the front wheels and an outrigger for the tail wheel. The two arms on the sides moved the platform in a half-circle up and down between the flight deck and the hangar deck.***

*Below: **Combining old and new aircraft manufacturing techniques, the Vindicator's front fuselage was clad in metal, while the rear was fabric covered. This is clearly visible in this formation shot of aircraft from VS-72.***

*Right: **A US Navy SB2U Vindicator (42-S-17) of VS-42 overflies its parent carrier, USS Ranger (CV-4), on 4 December 1941 during convoy escort duties in the Atlantic. Note that the wartime censor has deleted details under the forward fuselage of the aircraft.***

*Bottom right: **One of the seven Vought SB2U-3 Vindicators of VMSB-231 destroyed on the field at Ewa during the attack on Pearl Harbor, Oahu, Hawaii on 7 December 1941. All of VMSB-231's spares (the squadron was embarked in the USS Lexington, en route to Midway, at the time) were likewise destroyed.***

Chesapeake

The British Royal Navy took on stocks of Vindicators that were initially intended for France. Desperate for any and all war-making material, the British operated the Vindicator under the name of Chesapeake and installed British-centric equipment for better standardisation including additional machine guns and better armour protection. British Vindicators operated during 1941 but their performance limitations meant they were quickly relegated to training duties and eventually withdrawn from use.

Brewster XSBA-1/NAF SBN-1

Above: The first US Navy SBN-1 scout bomber (BuNo 1522) produced by the Naval Aircraft Factory, in flight over Washington DC on 12 February 1942. Manufactured between 1940 and 1942, the SBN was the production version of the XSBA-1 designed by Brewster in 1934. Never used in combat, the SBN served as a stateside trainer. The SBN illustrated is wearing the overall light grey pre-World War 2 camouflage used until October 1941.

The SBN was a short-lived three-seat mid-wing monoplane scout bomber/torpedo aircraft designed by the Brewster Aeronautical Corporation as the XSBA-1 and built under license by the Naval Aircraft Factory (NAF).

When the US Navy issued a specification for a scout-bomber (SB) in 1934, the Brewster Aeronautical Corporation was invited to submit a proposal. Its XSBA-1 was a mid-wing design incorporating an internal bomb bay. Brewster received a contract to build a single prototype in October 1934 and this took to the air for the first time on 15 April 1934 before being delivered to the Navy for evaluation. Early trials revealed less than expected performance but when the XSBA-1 reappeared in 1937 it had been modified and fitted with an uprated engine and three-bladed propeller, giving it a top speed of over 250mph, the fastest of any of the SB types tested by the US Navy at the time. Its crew of three (pilot, navigator and gunner) sat under a greenhouse-style canopy with good views of the surrounding action. The main landing gear retracted into the sides of the lower fuselage using a complex strut arrangement. The tail was capped by a single vertical tail fin and low-set horizontal tailplanes. Perforated split dive-flaps were installed on the mid-set wings to slow the descent of the aircraft when on its dive-bombing run. An internal bomb bay supported a single 500lb bomb. Power was served through a Wright XR-1820-22 Cyclone radial piston engine of 950hp giving it a range out to 1,015 miles and a service ceiling of 28,300ft.

Because of the pressures of producing and developing the Brewster F2A Buffalo, the company was unable to produce the

NAF SBN-1

Crew:	Three, pilot, navigator and gunner
Length:	27ft 8in (8.43m)
Wingspan:	39ft (11.89m)
Height:	8ft 7in (2.64m)
Loaded weight:	3,759lb (3,066kg)
Powerplant:	Wright R-1820-22 Cyclone radial engine of 950hp
Top speed:	254mph
Service ceiling:	28,300ft (8,600m)
Armament:	1× rearward-firing, flexible .30in (7.62mm) machine gun
Ordnance:	Up to 500lb (230kg) of bombs

aircraft and the US Navy acquired a license to manufacture the aircraft itself at the Naval Aircraft Factory. In September 1938, the Navy placed an order for 30 production aircraft. Due to pressures of work at the NAF, it did not deliver the first aircraft, now designated the SBN-1, until 1941; the remaining aircraft were delivered between June 1941 and March 1942.

By the time it was introduced in 1941, the 1930s-era machine was obsolete and proved of little value to foreseeable operations. SBN-1s served briefly with VB-3 of USS *Saratoga's* air group and were later used as trainers by VT-8 aboard USS *Hornet*. But the inevitable end was not far away and the type was ingloriously withdrawn from service from August 1942.

*Right: **The Brewster XSBA-1 at the NACA Langley Research Center, VA, on 17 May 1943. This prototype flew at Langley from 1939 until 1941 and returned a year later with a new wing, one that had increased dihedral. It flew in this form until leaving the NACA in September 1945.***

Grumman F4F Wildcat

Snub-nosed with a rotund fuselage and plank-like wings it was never going to win any beauty awards, but the Grumman F4F Wildcat proved there was more to an effective fighter than svelte looks. In fact, it is hard to see how Allied navies, particularly that of the USA, could have managed without the sturdy, pugnacious Wildcat. A typical product of the Grumman 'Iron Works,' the F4F could also hand out punishment as well as take it. Its battle honours were as good as they come: the Battle of the Atlantic, the heroic defence of Wake Island, Guadalcanal, the Battle of the Coral Sea and the Battle of Midway.

Although Leroy Grumman had only formed his eponymous aircraft manufacturing company at Bethpage Long Island in 1929 he quickly established a reputation as a respected builder of naval aircraft and by 1936 the latest in the line, the F3F, was serving with US Navy fighter squadrons. It was during that year that Grumman was invited to design a new monoplane fighter powered by the latest 900hp engines. Grumman began work on the XF4F-2 and the prototype flew for the first time in September 1937 with company test pilot Robert L. Hall at the controls. In December it was flown to Anacostia Naval Air Station for official evaluation alongside the rival Brewster and the Seversky NF-1, a naval adaptation of the Army's P-35. Engine trouble dogged Grumman's contender and it was the Brewster design that was awarded a production contract. Yet the team at Bethpage refused to give up on the design. The revised XF4F-3 had a bigger wing with square rather than rounded tips,

new tail surfaces and a more powerful engine with a two-stage supercharger. This developed 1,200hp rather than the previous 1,050. The nose-mounted guns had gone and instead there were two 0.5in Brownings in each wing. Cockpit armour was also specified.

The US Navy liked the F4F-3 so much that it ordered 285. It was to be a wise decision. The aircraft was in service by the time of the Japanese attack on Pearl Harbor in December 1941. By that time the new fighter had been officially named Wildcat.

Apart from the US Navy, France also ordered Grumman F4Fs under the company designation G-36A. For its 81 aircraft the French Navy specified Wright Cyclone engines and an armament of six wing-mounted 7.5mm Darne machine guns. With the fall of France the aircraft were diverted to the Royal Navy, which operated them as Martlet MkIs.

Meanwhile, production of the F4F-3 for the US Navy was proceeding in parallel. In April 1940 the third and fourth production aircraft were fitted with single-stage supercharged Cyclone engines after troubles were experienced with the two-stage Twin Wasp. These variants were designated F4F-5.

A further F4F-3 received a single-stage two-speed supercharged Twin Wasp to become the F4F-6, later re-designated F4F-3A of which 95 were delivered. The first 30 F4F-3As were released for delivery to Greece in the spring of 1941 but were also diverted to the Fleet Air Arm to operate as Martlet IIIs. Ten further F4F-3As were diverted from the US Navy to the FAA in lieu of the first of 100

of the next main Wildcat variant, the F4F-4. This incorporated changes resulting from RN combat experience particularly the addition of an additional pair of 0.5in machine guns. The next major production variant was the FM-1 of which 1,151 were produced. This was essentially the F4F-4 lightened to make it suitable for operation from the smaller escort carriers and was built by the Eastern Aircraft Division of General Motors.

By 1943 Grumman was going into production with the F6F Hellcat but Wildcats were still in demand. Eastern therefore started building what was to be the last of the breed but also the most numerous, the FM-2/Wildcat VI. It had started life as the XF4F-8 with a Cyclone engine and taller vertical tail. It remained in production until 1945.

Although the F4F was designed for the US Navy it was Royal Navy pilots who first unsheathed its claws in anger. On Christmas day 1940 a section of Martlets from No 804 Naval Air Squadron intercepted a Junkers Ju88 reconnaissance bomber over Scapa Flow, forcing it down.

That same month VF-4 took delivery of the US Navy's first F4F-3. The Marines had 61, but within minutes of the Japanese attack on Hawaii on 7 December 1941, VMF-211 lost nine

A US Navy Grumman F4F-4 Wildcat fighter taking off from the aircraft carrier USS Ranger (CV-4) to attack targets ashore during the invasion of Morocco, on 8 November 1942. Note the US Army observation aircraft in the left middle distance.

*Above: **As World War 2 approached, the once bright schemes applied to Wildcats became more drab. These three VMF-111 F4F-3s are seen during war manoeuvres and sport red crosses on the wings for identification purposes.***

of its Wildcats before they had a chance to leave the ground.

From December 1941 to the following June, the US Navy mustered five frontline fighter squadrons with just 138 pilots and operating from five carriers. For much of this period their efforts were concentrated on limiting the extent of the Japanese expansion, particularly in the south-west Pacific area. The Japanese, however, had the advantage with more carriers, experienced air crews and high quality aircraft. The deadly Zero fighter soon proved itself more than a match for its opponents. The US fighter pilots discovered that the Zero was faster,

turned tighter and climbed quicker and were forced to evolve tactics that would place them on more even terms.

However, the pugnacious, tubby fighters remained in demand as ground-support aircraft operating from escort carriers. Their finest hour came in October 1944 during the Battle of Leyte Gulf when on one day FM-2 Wildcat pilots claimed to have shot down 270 Japanese aircraft. The Wildcats were also involved in the

Iwo Jima and Okinawa operations so that by VJ day the pilots of FM Wildcats were credited with 432 aerial victories. In all, Wildcat pilots shot down a confirmed 905 enemy aircraft and suffered 178 aerial losses to achieve a kill to loss ratio of 6.9:1.

Although over 8,000 Wildcats were built, 6,000 were manufactured by General Motors, leaving the Grumman factory free to concentrate on the F4F's successor, the F6F Hellcat.

Above: **Three US Navy Grumman F4F-3/3A Wildcats of VF-5 from the aircraft carrier USS Yorktown (CV-5) flying in formation, circa 1941. Depending on the variant, the Wildcat/Martlet was powered by the 14-cylinder Pratt & Whitney Twin Wasp or nine-cylinder Wright Cyclone radial engine. The Cyclone was lighter and less complicated than the Twin Wasp but was noisier and vibrated more. It was also larger in diameter, resulting in a bigger cowling and consequent affect on forward vision from the cockpit.**

Above right: **The stubby XF4F-2 prototype flew for the first time in September 1937. The Wildcat was the only US Navy fighter to serve throughout World War 2 and the first to feature a two-stage supercharged engine, self-sealing fuel tanks and armour protection for the pilot.**

Centre right: **Generally considered roomy, the F4F's cockpit was covered by a framed aft-sliding hood and there was an armoured glass windscreen. There was a good view forward but virtually none to the rear.**

Right: **A US Navy Grumman F4F-4 Wildcat exhibited at Columbus Circle, New York City (USA) for bond selling purposes. Built around a single inclined main spar, the wings featured the Grumman-designed STO-Wing system. This enabled each outer section to be pivoted backwards to lie parallel with the fuselage rather than simply fold upwards and take up precious head-room in crowded hangar decks.**

Right: Wildcats on the prowl. The Zero was found to be superior to the Wildcat in speed and climb at all altitudes above 1,000ft (308m) as well as in service ceiling and dive. In a dive the two were virtually equal but the Zero's turning circle was much smaller and its stalling speed even lower. It was therefore considered foolhardy for Wildcat pilots to engage the Japanese fighter in a dogfight. Although the Wildcat was not as nimble as the Zero, it could take far more punishment than its Japanese foe. A total of 59 Wildcat pilots shot down five or more enemy aircraft and the three top-scoring aces all served with the US Marines during the battle for Guadalcanal in the Solomon Islands.

Below: Grumman F4F-4 Wildcats from VF-71 and RAF Supermarine Spitfire MkVcs of No 603 Squadron on the deck of the aircraft carrier USS Wasp (CV-7) on 19 April 1942. Having landed her torpedo planes and dive bombers at Hatson in Orkney, Wasp had loaded 47 Spitfires on 13 April, then departed on the 14th for Operation 'Calendar'. Wasp and her consorts passed through the Straits of Gibraltar under cover of the pre-dawn darkness on 19 April. At 04.00hrs on 20 April, Wasp launched 11 Wildcats to form a combat air patrol before the Spitfires departed for Malta. When the launch was complete, Wasp retired toward Gibraltar.

Bottom: A GM-built Grumman FM-2 Wildcat upended after a barrier crash on board USS Sable during pilot training in the Great Lakes, May 1945.

CF4F-4

Engine:	Pratt & Whitney R-1830-86.
Power:	1,200hp
Max speed:	320mph (510kph) at 18,000ft (5,538m)
Length:	28ft 9in (8.85m)
Wing span:	38ft (11.69m)
Height:	9ft 2.5in (2.83m)
Armament:	4x 0.50in (12.7mm) machine guns
Max loaded weight:	7,950lb (3,614kg)
Range:	770 miles (1,232km)

FM-2

Engine:	Wright R-1820-56 Cyclone.
Power:	1,350hp
Max speed:	332mph (531kph) at 28,800ft (8,862m)
Length:	28ft 9in (8.85m)
Wing span:	38ft (11.69m)
Height:	9ft 11in (3.05m)
Armament:	4x 0.50in (12.7mm) machine guns plus 2x 250lb (114kg) bombs or 6x 5in (12.7cm) rockets
Max loaded weight:	8,721lb (3,964kg)
Range:	900 miles (1,440km)

Wildcat Aces

Given the relatively small number of pilots involved and the intensity of the fighting in the first 12 months of the war in the Pacific, there was no shortage of Wildcat aces.

A total of 25 US Navy and 34 USMC F4F pilots were credited with shooting down five or more enemy aircraft and therefore became aces. The first of them was Lt (jg) Edward 'Butch' O'Hare of VF-3 who was credited with shooting down five Mitsubishi G4M 'Betty' bombers in a single engagement in February 1942.

During the Battle of Midway three further F4F pilots became aces. Lt Cdr John S. Hatch CO of VF-3 took his total score to 6.5 as did the battle's top-scorer, VF-3's Lt (jg) Scott 'Doc' McCuskey. The Navy's top-scoring F4F pilot was Donald E. Runyon of VF-6 who shot down eight enemy aircraft during three engagements in August 1942.

The Guadalcanal fighting resulted in 30 USMC aces including the war's top three Wildcat pilots. Between them VMF-223, VMF-121 and VMF-224 claimed to have downed 315 Japanese aircraft. Maj Joseph J. Foss had 26 victories, Maj John L. Smith 19 and Maj Marion E. Carl 16.5. All three survived the war.

The first US Navy ace of World War 2, Lt Edward Butch O'Hare seated in the cockpit of his Wildcat circa spring 1942. The aircraft is marked with five Japanese flags, representing the five enemy bombers he was credited with shooting down. He was killed in November 1943 when he was shot down by friendly fire.

A sequence of images that illustrate the inherent dangers of carrier operations. The Wildcat was generally considered to have superb deck landing characteristics with a slow approach speed and good visibility forward. Although its undercarriage was of narrow track it was capable of absorbing very heavy landings… but during times of conflict accidents were inevitable. Here, the pilot of F4F-4 Wildcat White F4 is fighting vainly to save his aircraft before it careers off the deck, presumably having missed the wires. The ack ack gunners take evasive action as the wingtip hits their position and breaks off. The pilot quickly clambers out of the cockpit after the aircraft meets its inevitable fate. White F4 was the mount of double ace Lt C. R. 'Skull' Stimpson of VF-11 'Sundowners' at Guadalcanal in the summer of 1943 (when this incident occurred), though it is not known if he was at the controls at this time.

Grumman F4F Wildcat of VF-42, US Navy, aboard the USS Ranger.

Grumman F4F-3 Wildcat flown by Maj R. E. Galer of VMF-224, US Marine Corps, on Guadalcanal, summer 1942. Maj Galer was one of the top scoring aces of the Guadalcanal campaign and the fourth top Wildcat ace with 13 kills.

Grumman FM-2 Wildcat flown by Lt Leo M. Freko of VC-4, US Navy, aboard USS White Plains circa 1944.

Brewster F2A-3

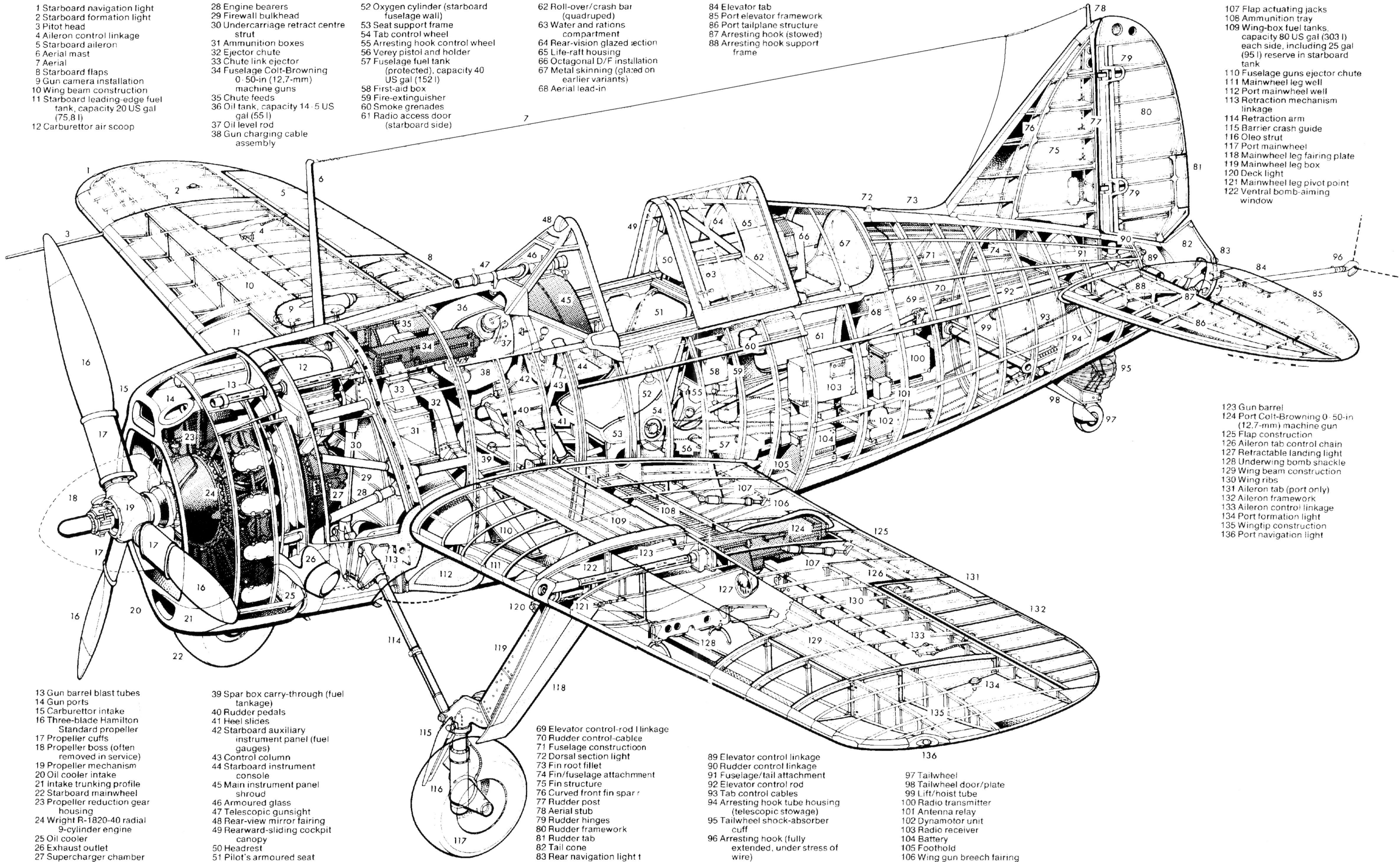

Grumman F4F-4 Wildcat

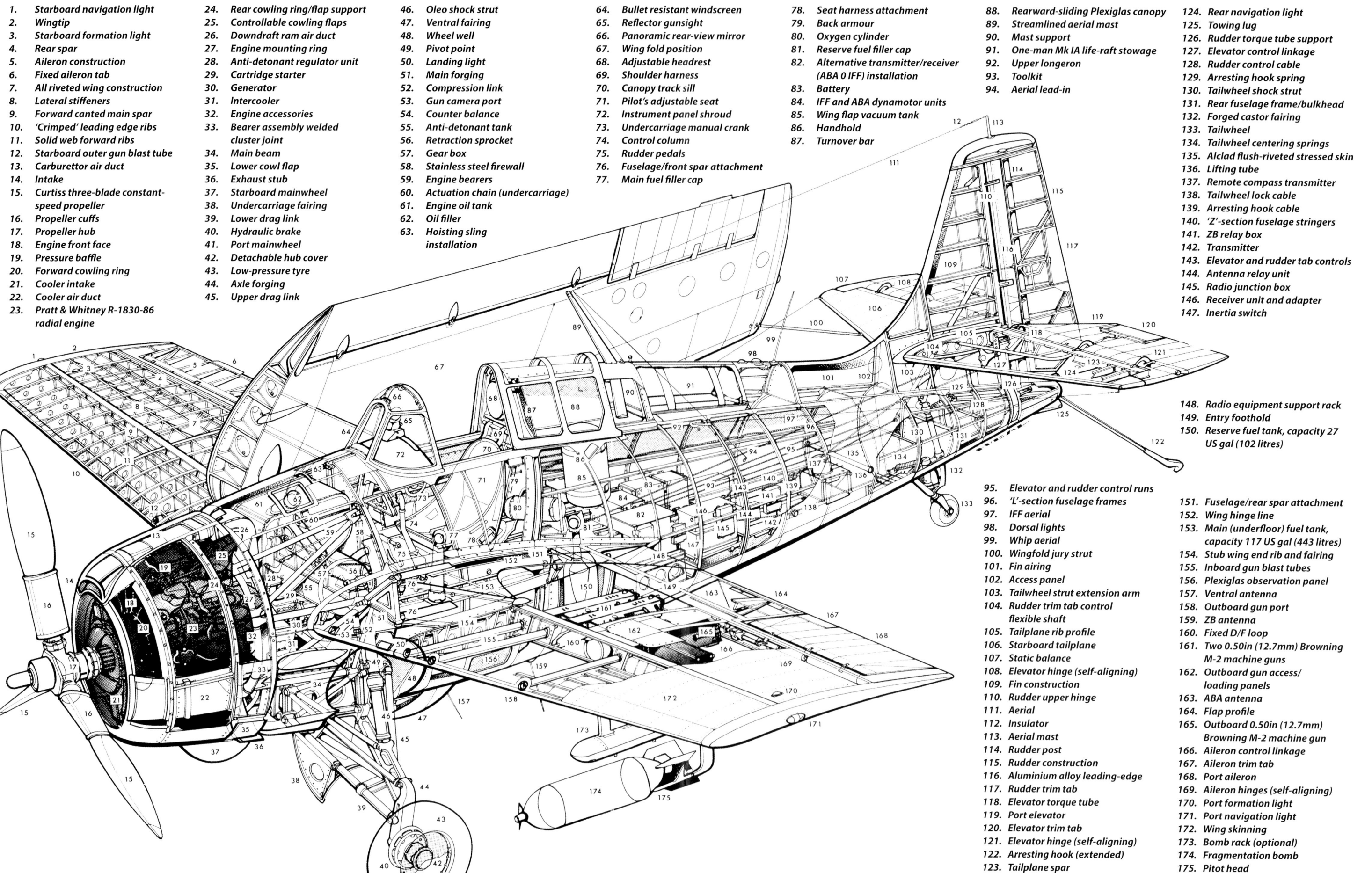

Brewster F2A Buffalo

The infamous Brewster F2A Buffalo was the first US Navy monoplane fighter and one of the first of the 'modern breed' available when the US entered the war. However, the stubby aircraft was not liked by its pilots and when the aircraft came up against vastly superior opposition, it was quickly dubbed 'the Flying Coffin'.

In 1935, the US Navy issued a requirement for a carrier-based fighter intended to replace the Grumman F3F biplane. The Brewster XF2A-1 monoplane, designed by a team led by Dayton T. Brown, was one of two aircraft designs that were initially considered and first flew on 2 December 1937. Early tests were promising and in June 1938 production of the F2A-1 was begun at the Brewster Building in Long Island City, NY.

The design of the Brewster Buffalo was fundamental in every sense of the word, with the four fixed 12.7mm machine guns being the only true saving grace of the machine. The new Brewster fighter had a modern look with a compact fuselage, mid-set monoplane wings and a host of advanced features. It was all-metal, with flush-riveted, stressed aluminium construction, although control surfaces were still fabric-covered. Powered by the 940hp (701kW) Wright R-1820-34 engine, production aircraft were much heavier than the prototype reducing the initial rate of climb to 2,600ft/min. Plagued by production difficulties, Brewster delivered only 11 F2A-1s to the US Navy.

The updated F2A-2, of which the US Navy ordered 43, included a more powerful R-1820-40 engine, a better propeller, and integral flotation gear, but still lacked pilot armour and self-sealing tanks. The increase in engine power was welcomed, but to some extent offset by the increased loaded weight of the aircraft, while top speed was increased to a respectable 323mph. Pilots initially praised the good turning and manoeuvring abilities of the aircraft, but already there were fears that it was rapidly becoming obsolete. Meanwhile, Brewster produced the F2A-3, conceived as a long-range reconnaissance fighter with a new wet wing with self-sealing features and a larger fuselage tank, which provided increased fuel capacity and protection,

Above: The Brewster XF2A-1 prototype during testing. Although initial performance of the aircraft was promising, production examples were much heavier because of an increase in armament and handling suffered greatly as a result.

but also increased the aircraft's weight. The addition of armour plating for the pilot and increased ammunition capacity further increased the aircraft's weight, resulting in a reduced top speed and rate of climb, while substantially degrading the Brewster's turning and manoeuvring capability. By this time, the Navy had become disenchanted with the Buffalo, and had become annoyed at frequent production delays. Now considered a second line fighter, a number were transferred to the US Marine Corps, which deployed two F2A-3 squadrons to the Pacific, one at Palmyra Atoll and another at Midway Island. VMF-221 was the only US unit to use the F2A in combat, and was outmatched by the faster, more manoeuvrable Japanese Zero. Of the 23 Brewster Buffaloes in the Battle of Midway, only 10 returned. After only a few months of active duty, the F2A Brewster Buffalo was replaced by the F4F Wildcat and the remaining aircraft were put to use as advanced trainers. The introduction in late 1943 of vastly superior American carrier-borne fighters such as the F6F Hellcat and Vought F4U Corsair soon relegated the Brewster F2A-3 to a distant, if painful memory.

Buffalo overseas

Several nations, including Finland, Belgium, Britain and the Netherlands ordered the Buffalo. It was the RAF that gave the aircraft its 'Buffalo' name, but experiences showed that it was unfit for duty in western Europe. The aircraft were sent to RAF, RAAF and RNZAF squadrons in the Far East where it found modest success before suffering high casualties at the hands of the more agile Japanese fighters over Burma.

Meanwhile, Finland proved to be the only successful user of the Brewster F2A Buffalo, receiving the original lighter version and fighting off wave after wave of Soviet aggression during three years of the Russo-Finnish War. In service from 1941 to 1945, Buffalos of Lentolaivue 24 (Fighter Squadron 24) claimed 477 Soviet Air Force warplanes destroyed, with the combat loss of just 19 Buffalos, an outstanding victory ratio of 26:1.

Buffalos of No 453 Squadron RAAF lined up at RAF Sembawang in November 1941. Buffalo AN185/TD-V was flown by Flt Lt Doug Vanderfield, who shot down three Japanese bombers (two Ki-48s and one Ki-51) over Butterworth, Penang on 13 December 1941, while his undercarriage was still down.

*Above: **Initially US pilots liked the Buffalo, but soon noticed that the wheel struts sometimes broke, that the engine leaked oil, and that the guns sometimes didn't fire. And when they flew it against the nimble fighters of Japan, too often they didn't come back.***

*Right: **A US Navy Brewster F2A-3 fighter pictured during a training flight from NAS Miami, FL, on 2 August 1942. At the controls is Lt Cdr Joseph C. Clifton who later flew a captured A6M2 Zero, obtaining valuable technical data that was used to refine fighter tactics against the Japanese.***

*Far right: **A US Navy Brewster F2A-2 Buffalo at the NACA Langley Research Center, Hampton, VA, on 9 February 1943.***

Douglas SBD Dauntless

Very few aircraft have had such an impact on World history as the Douglas SBD Dauntless dive-bomber. It possessed long range, good handling characteristics, manoeuvrability, potent bomb load, great diving characteristics, good defensive armament and ruggedness. But the SBD is best remembered as the bomber that delivered the fatal blows to the Japanese carriers at the Battle of Midway in June 1942 in one of the most decisive actions of World War 2.

The Dauntless originated with the design of the Northrop BT-1, Northrop Corporation then being a subsidiary of The Douglas Aircraft Corporation. Northrop was dissolved on 8 September 1937 and its designs continued production under the Douglas moniker. The new aircraft was a low-wing cantilever configuration of all-metal construction, except for fabric covered flight controls. By late 1937 numerous major modifications were ordered of the BT-1, one of which was the landing gear being changed from retracting backwards

into large fairing trousers beneath the wings, to folding laterally into recessed wheel wells. The new model, the XBT-2, provided the basis of the SBD Dauntless, which was developed at the Douglas El Segundo, CA plant. Both the US Marine Corps and Navy placed orders for the new dive-bomber, designated SBD-1 and SBD-2 respectively. Deliveries began in late 1940.

Capabilities for the SBD were adequate considering the type, with power derived from the single Wright-brand R-1820 series air-cooled engine rated at over 1,000hp (and achieving progressively better returns as new engines were introduced throughout its production life). Top speeds of 250mph could be reached along with a ceiling of just around 25,500ft with a range of well over 1,000 miles. The glazed cockpit could accommodate two

Left: A US Marine Corps Douglas SBD-6 Dauntless from VMSB-231 'Ace of Spades' flying from Majuro Atoll in early 1944. The markings indicate 23 bombing missions having been flown by the aircraft. The pilot of the aircraft is Maj Elmer G. Glidden, a Midway and Guadalcanal veteran, and commander of VMSB-231.

Left: Battle-scarred Douglas SBD Dauntless dive-bombers in formation over an unidentified atoll in the Pacific Ocean. The Dauntless saw action in the Battle of Coral Sea and the Battle of Midway (sinking four Japanese aircraft carriers), working side-by-side with TBD Devastator torpedo elements to form a deadly one-two punch, with cover provided by F4F Wildcat fighters.

Below: A US Navy Douglas SBD Dauntless in a bombing dive using its characteristic dive flap.

Bottom: Dauntless dive-bombers of VB-16 off USS Lexington (CV-16) fly low over Japanese installations on Param Island, Truk Atoll, 17-18 February 1944. VB-16 operated from Lexington during the period September 1943-June 1944, and was for a time one of only two Dauntless squadrons assigned to Pacific fleet carriers. The squadron participated in the famous attack against the Japanese Fleet during the Battle of the Philippine Sea in June 1944.

personnel – the pilot in a forward area and the gunner in a rear cockpit, seated back-to-back. The rear cockpit contained a trainable gun position (7.62mm type machine guns) and played a major defensive role in the survival of many an SBD and its crew. The pilot doubled as the bombardier and also aimed fixed-forward guns, which (eventually) would feature two 12.7mm (.50 calibre) heavy machine guns. A distinguishing feature of the wings were the large perforated dive flaps. The empennage was a traditional assembly with a single vertical tail surface. All of this was designed to carry a substantial bomb load that could be supplanted by depth charges if need be.

The SBD-3 (A-24-DE) was the first fully combat ready version with a total production of 585 airplanes, but the definitive SBD model was the SBD-5, which sported the more powerful R-1820-60 series radial and an increase in total ammunition. It was produced to the tune of some 3,000 examples. Along with the base SBD models, the Dauntless was also used as a photographic reconnaissance platform and designated with the appropriate 'P'.

At the time of the attack of Pearl Harbor, the Dauntless was the standard dive bomber and was the first US Navy aircraft to sink an enemy ship (Japanese sub I-70) in World War 2, just three days after the US entered the conflict. The first real test came on 7 May 1942, when US aircraft carriers, USS Lexington and USS Yorktown, faced three Japanese carriers in the Battle of the Coral Sea. The two-day battle was the first naval battle in which victory was decided by aircraft alone. Dauntless dive-bombers fought well alongside other US aircraft and were credited with 40 of the 91 enemy aircraft downed. During the battle, the US lost the carrier USS Lexington and the Japanese lost the light carrier Shoho, which was sunk by Dauntless and Devastator bombers. The Shokaku also received serious bomb damage and Zuikaku's air group was badly depleted, eliminating these carriers from the upcoming Midway operation.

In the great Battle of Midway in June, US naval aircraft, spearheaded by Dauntless dive-bombers, sank the Japanese carriers, Akagi, Kaga, and Soryu. Only the Hiryu remained operational which would launch a retaliatory strike against the USS Yorktown later in the day. However, before the day ended, US carrier dive-bombers found and attacked Hiryu, putting her out of action. A Japanese cruiser and 250 aircraft were also destroyed, for the loss of one US carrier, a destroyer and 150 aircraft. The Battle of Midway turned the tide of war against the Japanese in the Pacific.

As the war went on, the Dauntless equipped no less than 20 Marine squadrons and were retained until late 1944. It was the main type US navy dive-bomber and was not only used in the Pacific, but also during the Allied landings

in North Africa and in the Battle of the Atlantic. The Dauntless had the lowest attrition rate of any US carrier aircraft, because of its ability to absorb battle damage. Dauntless aircraft accounted for many Japanese aircraft shot down in air-to-air combat, and finished their wartime career as anti-submarine bombers and as attack aircraft, carrying depth charges and rocket projectiles respectively.

The Dauntless was one of the most important aircraft in the Pacific War, sinking more enemy shipping in the region than any other Allied bomber. Its battle record shows that in addition to six Japanese carriers, 14 enemy cruisers had been sunk, along with six destroyers, 15 transports or cargo ships and scores of various lesser craft.

By the time Dauntless production ended in 1944, a staggering 5,938 had been built. By then, the US Navy had begun replacing the type with the more powerful SB2C Helldiver.

Douglas SBD Dauntless

Crew:	Two, pilot and gunner
Length:	33ft 1in (10.09m)
Wingspan:	41ft 6in (12.66m)
Height:	13ft 7in (4.14m)
Empty weight:	6,404lb (2,905kg)
Loaded weight:	9,359lb (4,245kg)
Powerplant:	Wright R-1820-60 radial engine of 1,200hp (895kW)
Top speed:	255mph at 14,000ft
Service ceiling:	25,530ft (7,780m)
Armament:	2× 0.50in (12.7mm) forward-firing synchronised Browning M2 machine guns in engine cowling, 2× 0.30in (7.62mm) flexible-mounted Browning machine guns in rear
Ordnance:	2,250lb (1,020kg) of bombs

Right: **A US Navy Dauntless (BuNo 4542), of USS Enterprise's VB-6, is parked on board USS Yorktown (CV-5) after landing at about 11.40hrs on 4 June 1942 during the Battle of Midway. This aircraft, damaged during the attack on the Japanese aircraft carrier Kaga that morning, landed on Yorktown as it was low on fuel. It was later lost with the carrier.**

Centre right: **A Dauntless of VB-6 crashes into the catwalk after catching an arrestor wire on the aircraft carrier USS Enterprise (CV-6) during operations in the Pacific, in early 1942.**

Far right: **A damaged SBD-2 of VB-6 on the flight deck of the aircraft carrier USS Enterprise (CV-6), 1 February 1942. Withdrawing after launching an attack against Kwajalein Atoll, Enterprise was attacked by five Japanese Mitsubishi G4M 'Betty' land-based bombers. Manning the flexible rear machine gun on an SBD-2 of bombing squadron VB-6, AMM Bruno Gaido attempted to help fight off the attackers. The wing of one of the disabled bombers severed the tail of Gaido's Dauntless, spreading burning gasoline across the deck before crashing into the ocean. For his heroism, Gaido was promoted and assigned duty as an aircrewman. Gaido was shot down with his pilot Ensign Frank W. O'Flaherty on 4 June 1942 and later picked up by the Japanese destroyer Makigumo. Circa 8-9 June both were tied to water-filled gasoline drums and dumped overboard.**

Right: **A VB-10 Dauntless in the landing pattern above the aircraft carrier USS Enterprise (CV-6) during operations in the Pacific. Note the bomb rack and YE radar antenna beneath the starboard wing. One of the last two SBD squadrons to operate from US fleet carriers during World War 2, VB-10 participated in the Battle of the Philippine Sea on 19-20 June 1944.**

Below: **A US Navy launch officer on board USS Lexington (CV-16) signals the launch of a Douglas SBD-5 Dauntless of VB-16 on a strike in the Central Pacific. The squadron participated in the famous attack against the Japanese Fleet during the Battle of the Philippine Sea in June 1944.**

Operation 'Leader' was the code name for an attack
undertaken by aircraft from the carrier USS Ranger on
4 October 1943 on German shipping along the coast of
Norway in the Bodø area. The task force reached launch
position off the Vestfjorden before dawn completely
undetected. At 06.18hrs USS Ranger launched 20 SBD
Dauntless dive-bombers and an escort of eight F4F
Wildcat fighters. One division of dive-bombers attacked
the 8,000-ton freighter La Plata, while the rest continued
north to attack a German ship convoy. The bombers
severely damaged a tanker and a smaller troop transport
and sank two small German merchant ships.
Painting by Mark Postlethwaite/www.posart.com

MARK POSTLETHWAITE GAvA '07

Chance Vought F4U Corsair

While the Grumman F6F Hellcat had a huge impact on the war in the Pacific, the Vought F4U Corsair raised the bar significantly. When compared to the Hellcat or Japan's Mitsubishi A6M Zero, it dominated the stats. It was the fastest, heaviest and had the highest service ceiling that led to its superiority. Its capacity to dive at a very high speed, combined with its firepower, meant that the lightly armoured Japanese fighters and bombers never knew what hit them.

The Grumman Aircraft Corporation was the dominant designer and producer of US Navy aircraft in the 1940s and into the 1950s. The F4F Wildcat was considered to be the best fighter in the Pacific during the early stages of World War 2, followed shortly by the F6F Hellcat that racked up an unbelievable score all the way through to the end of the conflict. However, back in the late 1930s the US Navy had put out a request to several aircraft companies for a fighter that could match anything Germany or Japan had. At that time, Japan was a complete unknown except in terms of what had appeared over China, so most of Grumman's efforts were focused on fighter aircraft that the Germans were known to possess.

In 1938, aircraft designer Rex Biesel came up with an unusual prototype, the XF4U-1, powered by an XR-2800-4 prototype of the Pratt & Whitney Double Wasp twin-row 18-cylinder radial engine, rated at 1,805hp. When it was rolled out, the XF4U had the biggest and most powerful engine, largest propeller and probably the largest wing of any fighter in history. In order to give the propeller sufficient ground clearance, it also famously featured an inverted gullwing design. The first flight of the XF4U-1 was made on 29 May 1940, with Lyman A. Bullard Jr at the controls. The maiden flight proceeded normally until a hurried landing was made when the elevator trim tabs failed because of flutter. A rather inauspicious start for what was to become one of the best-known and feared fighters in the world – the famous F4U Corsair.

As with any new fighter design, there were problems early on. It was originally planned as a carrier-based fighter, but initial trial operations produced less than desired results. There was serious trouble with stalling and the pilot's forward visibility was very poor due to the long nose. The angle the Corsair had to adopt on approach and take-off made it difficult for even the most experienced pilots. With these early problems, the land-based US Marine Corps received the bulk of the early Corsairs and quickly racked up impressive scores against Japanese Zeros. Most of these pilots, who had transitioned from the F4F Wildcat on to the Corsair, claimed it put them in a position to dominate the Zero in dogfights.

The F4U required a very powerful engine to drive the massive Hamilton Standard Hydromatic three-blade propeller. The early models used the Pratt & Whitney R-2800 powerplant, which evolved to produce 2,100hp. As the more powerful engines were developed, a new four-blade prop was installed which added more speed and ordnance-carrying ability.

Due to the unique configuration of the Corsair's wings, the landing gear had to be very rigid, which posed a serious problem when undergoing carrier evaluation. With the long nose, the forward visibility of the pilot was reduced, and when trying to drop in and catch the arresting wire the F4U tended to bounce, causing it to miss. The problem was solved when the strut's air pressure was increased and the gear's Schrader valve was replaced.

The original prototype had two .50in (12.7mm) machine guns mounted in the nose, but these were quickly removed when production of the F4U-1 began. The standard package for most of the Corsairs was six 0.5in Browning machine guns that carried a total of 2,350 rounds. In August 1943, a new version started coming off the line that would have four 20mm long-barrelled Hispano cannon protruding forward of the leading edge of the wings. However, the 0.50in version would be the most widely used in the Pacific.

*Right: **F4U-1A white 29 of Lt (jg) Ira C. Kepford of VF-17, in early 1944. 'Ike' Kepford was the US Navy's most successful Corsair pilot with 16 confirmed victories, one probable and one damaged. He was awarded the DFC for outstanding skill during operations in the New Georgia area between 27 October and 1 December 1943.***

F4U-1 and FG-1

Crew:	One
Length:	33ft 8in (10.2m)
Wingspan:	41ft (12.5m)
Height:	14ft 9in (4.5m)
Empty weight:	9,205lb (4,174kg)
Loaded weight:	14,669lb (6,653kg)
Powerplant:	Pratt & Whitney R-2800 of 2,000hp
Top speed:	417mph at 19,500ft
Service ceiling:	41,500ft (12,649m)
Armament:	6x 0.50in machine guns, 400 rounds per gun
Ordnance:	One 1,000lb bomb (2x 500lb) or 8x 5in rockets

The Corsair pilot had very poor forward visibility on landing and take-off. This was made worse in the very early F4U-1s when the cockpit had to be moved back 3ft to maintain the centre of gravity when the self-sealing fuel tank was installed. The number of frames in the canopy was reduced to improve the pilot's vision and it was made jettisonable at the same time. The RAF made several changes in the F4U including installing the 'Malcolm hood' canopy, which gave an excellent view out. Later models of the Corsair would all have this clear canopy with its bubble-shaped top.

The main competitor for the Corsair in the Pacific was the deadly Japanese Zero. The skill of the American pilots in the F4F Wildcat had already taken a toll on enemy pilots and when the tough F4U began tangling with them they lost many more. Anytime the Marine or Navy Corsair pilots had the altitude advantage with their blinding diving speed combined with awesome firepower, there was no way for the Zero or any other Japanese aircraft to escape. Legend has it that the Japanese referred to the Corsair as 'Whistling Death' (for the noise made by airflow through the wing root-mounted oil cooler air intakes), but this was probably a story invented by the media.

By the end of the war in the Pacific, the F4U had established itself as a legend in aerial combat. At this time, just about every aircraft carrier was equipped with the latest Corsair models. The final figures released by the US Navy after the war confirmed that the gull-winged fighter had destroyed 2,140 enemy aircraft in aerial combat – while doing this, the F4U had only lost 189 aircraft in this same arena. From 13 February 1942 until August 1945, Corsairs logged 64,051 sorties, including 54,470 flown from land bases and 9,581 from carriers. These figures included both Navy and Marine operations.

By the end of World War Two, Vought had built and delivered 1,912 F4U-4s. It would be another seven years before the production line would shut down, the longest production run for any US prop fighter type. From the time the first airframe rolled off the line until the final example, the Corsair had undergone 981 major modifications and some 20,000 minor changes, but the basic airframe remained unaltered.

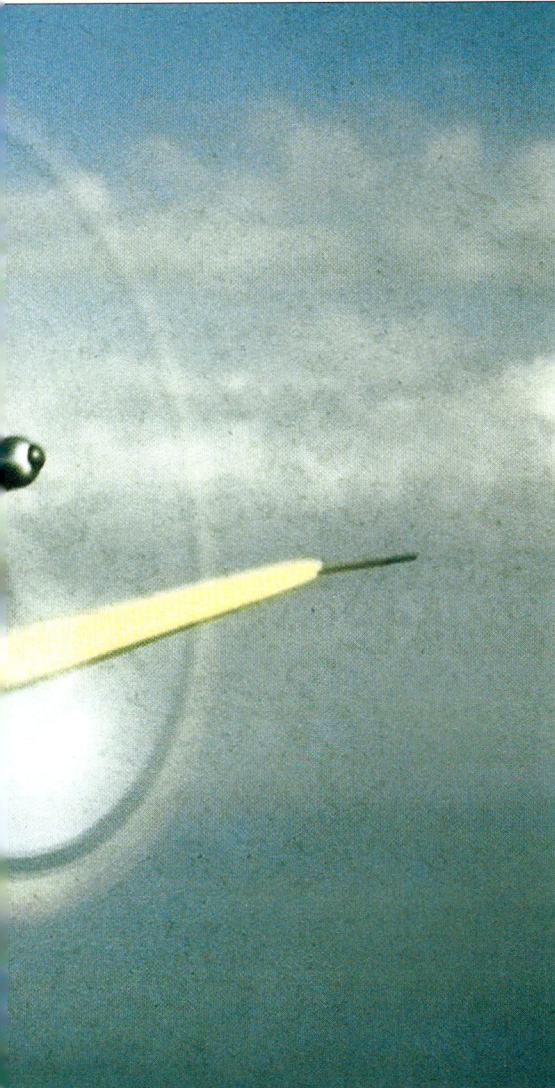

Left: The first Vought XF4U-1 is shown on an early test flight in 1940. This aircraft was the first US fighter to exceed 400mph in level flight when it achieved 404mph on 1 October 1940. The distinctive inverted gull-wing of the Corsair makes the type immediately identifiable.

Below: A Corsair pilot climbs aboard his steed in 1943. Interestingly, the pilot is clad in a leather CFN-24 electrically-heated flight suit, often worn during night missions.

Left: With its restricted view over its long nose, landing a Corsair on a carrier was always a challenge. Here an F4U-1 of VF-17 traps the wire on USS Charger (CVE-30) in spectacular but successful style in 1943.

Right: Corsairs as far as the eye can see. The impressive F4U Corsair production line of the Chance Vought aircraft factory in Connecticut during World War 2, which produced over 6,000 of the 'bent wing bird'.

Below: To the soundtrack of Pratt & Whitneys, F4U-2 Corsair night fighters from VFN-101 operate aboard the aircraft carrier USS Intrepid (CV-11) during the Marshall Islands campaign in early 1944.

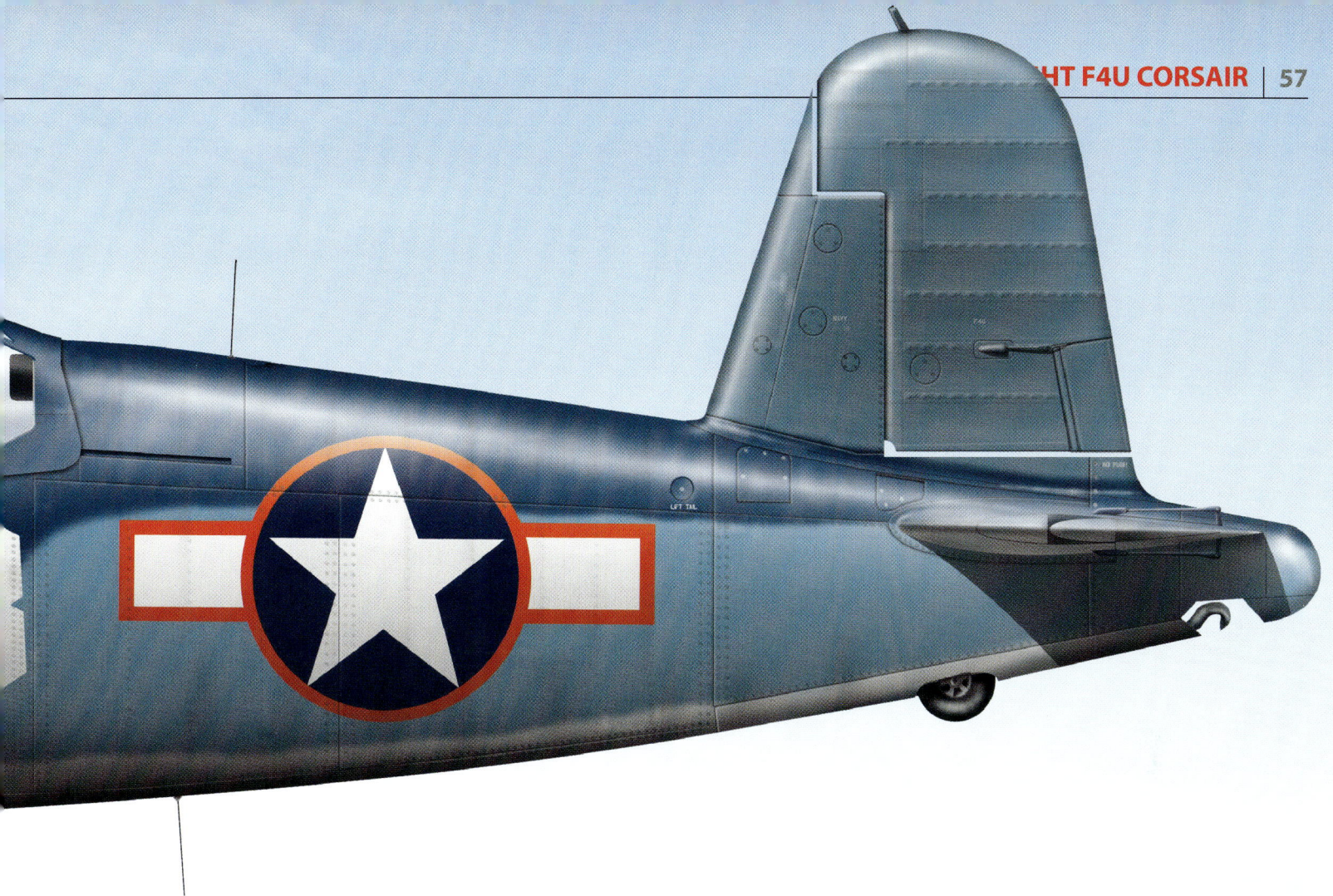

*Above: **Chance Vought F4U-1A Corsair flown by Ensign F. J. Streig of VF-17, US Navy, Bougainville circa 1944.** Rolando Ugolini/Airlinerart*

*Far left: **Supremely confident in their aircraft, US Navy pilots of VF-89 demonstrate the art of close formation flying. When the F4U was unleashed in the Pacific, it did not take long for the aircraft to begin exacting a heavy toll on the Japanese pilots.***

*Left: **A USMC F4U-1 Corsair looses its load of FFAR rocket projectiles on a run against a Japanese stronghold on Okinawa. In the lower background is the smoke of battle as Marine units advance in June 1945.***

*Below left: **The famous 'Ole 122', a Chance Vought F4U-1 of VMF-111, 'Devil Dogs', completed 100 dive-bombing missions against Japanese positions of the Marshall Islands.***

*Below: **The capture of Iwo Jima in early 1945 proved to be a safe haven for hundreds of battle-damaged aircraft that could not make it back to their base or carrier. These F4U-1Ds are lined up on Iwo with many other aircraft types in the background.***

Corsair Ace

US Marine Corps squadron VMF-124 was the first Marine squadron to take the F4U into combat. One of its pilots, Lt Kenneth A. Walsh, proved to be amongst the top-scoring Marine Corsair aces in the war with 21 confirmed kills. The unit arrived at Henderson Field, Guadalcanal on the morning of 12 February 1943 with 12 F4Us, and by the middle of August Walsh had already become a double ace with 10 kills. Later in the month he was involved in one of the most exciting dogfights to take place in the Pacific theatre, for which he would receive the Medal of Honor for his fighting prowess.

US Navy Vought F4U-1A Corsairs of VF-17 'Jolly Rogers' in the Southwest Pacific, possibly over Bougainville in early March 1944. White 29 is BuNo 55995, flown by Lt (jg) Ira C. Kepford, then the US Navy's leading ace, with 16 kills. Pilot of white 8 is thought to be Hal Jackson, while No 3, flown by Jim Streig, has an odd 'star and bar' insignia, perhaps with the red outline that was replaced with blue the previous summer.

VOUGHT CORSAIR
(F4U-1D)

One 2,000–h.p. air-cooled Pratt & Whitney Wasp

WING SPAN: 41 feet

LENGTH: 33 ft. 4 in.

HEIGHT: 16 ft. 1 in.

TOP SPEED: over 400 m.p.h.

RANGE: 1,700 miles

SERVICE CEILING: 35,000 feet

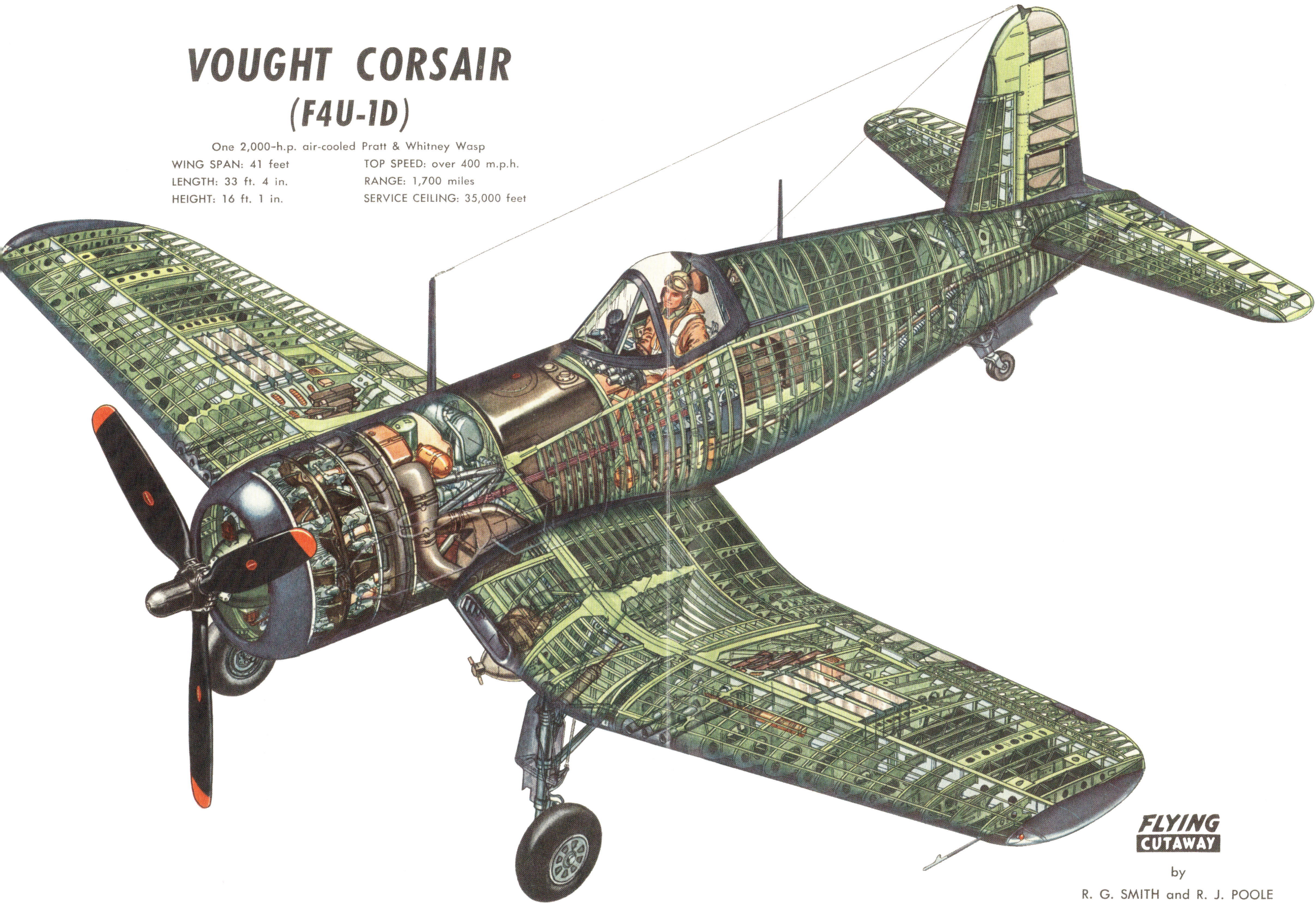

FLYING CUTAWAY

by

R. G. SMITH and R. J. POOLE

© July, 1945

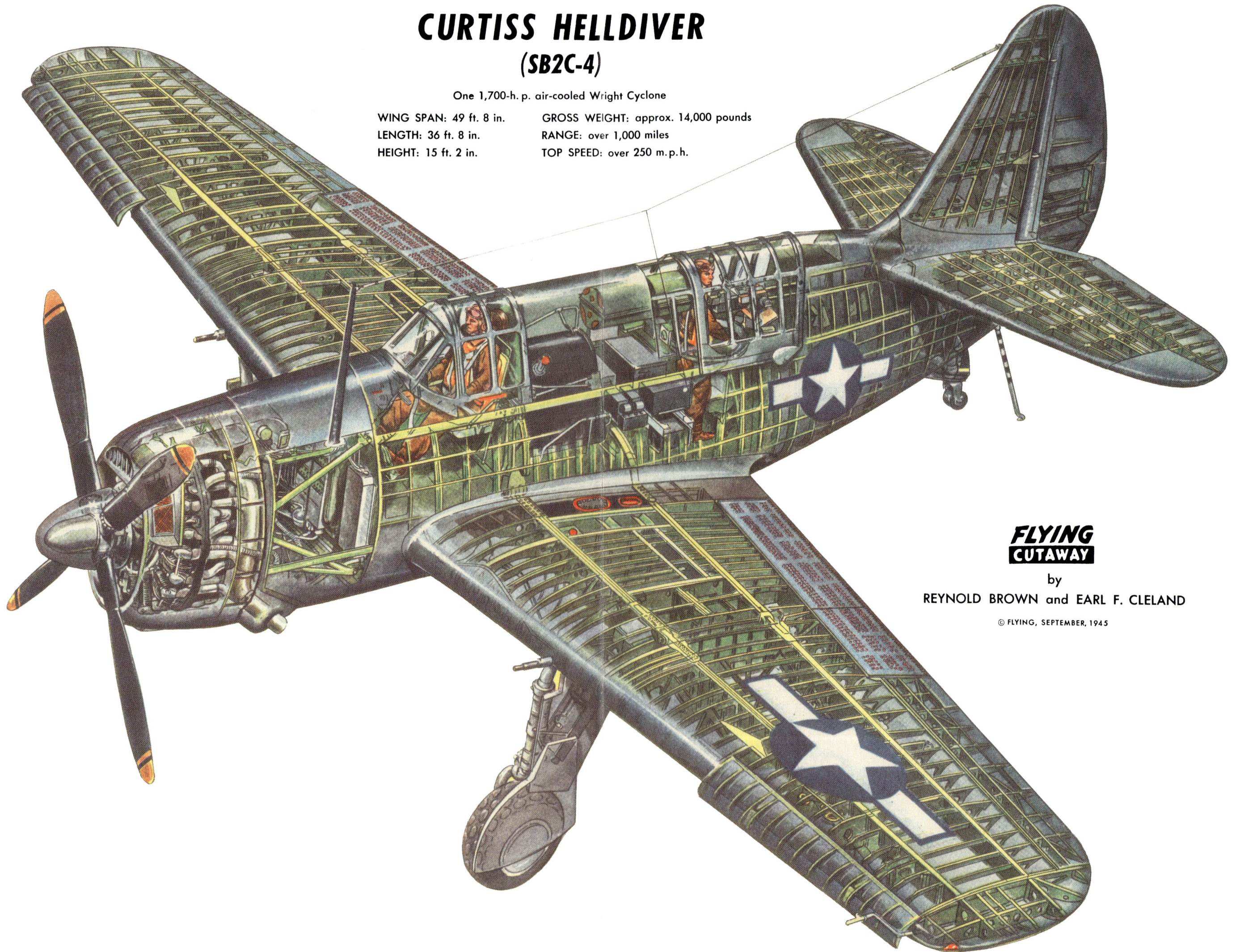

CURTISS HELLDIVER
(SB2C-4)

One 1,700-h.p. air-cooled Wright Cyclone

WING SPAN: 49 ft. 8 in.

LENGTH: 36 ft. 8 in.

HEIGHT: 15 ft. 2 in.

GROSS WEIGHT: approx. 14,000 pounds

RANGE: over 1,000 miles

TOP SPEED: over 250 m.p.h.

FLYING CUTAWAY

by

REYNOLD BROWN and EARL F. CLELAND

© FLYING, SEPTEMBER, 1945

Curtiss SB2C Helldiver

The 'Big-Tailed Beast' (or just 'Beast') and 'Son-of-a-Bitch 2nd Class' (after its designation) were just some of the derogatory names given to the Curtiss SB2C Helldiver by its crews. Tough to fly, poorly designed, and delivered too slowly, the early models of the Curtiss SB2C did not endear themselves to the US Navy, but eventually the Helldiver proved a most potent mount and was able to carry a greater ordnance payload than its predecessor.

The Helldiver was developed to replace the Douglas SBD Dauntless. It was a much larger aircraft, able to operate from the latest aircraft carriers and carry a considerable array of armament. It featured an internal bomb bay that reduced drag when carrying heavy ordnance. Saddled with demanding requirements set forth by both the US Marines and United States Army Air Forces, the manufacturer incorporated features of a 'multi-role' aircraft into the design, built around the Wright R-2600-8 engine. So anxious was the Navy for a modern dive-bomber, it gambled on Curtiss' reputation and placed an order for 200, even before the prototype flew on 18 December 1940. It crashed on 8 February 1941 when its engine failed on approach, but with the pressure to keep moving Curtiss was asked to rebuild it. The fuselage was

lengthened and a larger tail was fitted, while an autopilot was fitted as a result of the aircraft's poor stability. The revised prototype flew again on 20 October 1941, but was destroyed when its wing failed during diving tests on 21 December 1941, its test pilot, B.T. Hulse, parachuting to safety.

Large-scale production had already been ordered on 29 November 1940, but a large number of modifications were specified for the production model. The size of the fin and rudder was enlarged, fuel capacity was increased, self-sealing fuel tanks were added and the fixed armament was doubled to four 0.50in (12.7mm) machine guns in the wings, compared with the prototype's two cowling guns. The SB2C-2 was built with larger fuel tanks, improving its range considerably. But the programme suffered so many delays that the SB2C struggled to stay in the game. Since Curtiss' main plant in Buffalo, NY, was dedicated to the P-40, the company opened a new facility in Columbus, OH, just for the Helldiver. Curtiss also arrange for two Canadian companies to license-build the type. The first production Helldivers rolled off the line in June, 1942.

The Helldiver first saw combat with bombing squadron VB-17 from the carrier *Bunker Hill*

during an attack on Rabaul on 11 November 1943, nearly three years after the first flight of the prototype. In contrast, Grumman's TBF Avenger prototype had flown for the first time on 23 December 1941, and the first TBF-1 squadron had gone into action at the Battle of Midway, less than six months later. The Curtiss dive-bomber's debut with the fleet was less than promising. Although the Helldiver had originally been intended to exceed the performance parameters of the Dauntless by a wide margin, the early prognosis of the 'Beast' was unfavourable. The litany of faults that the Helldiver bore included the fact that it was underpowered, had a shorter range than the SBD, was equipped with an unreliable electrical system and was often poorly manufactured. The solution to these problems began with the introduction of the SB2C-3 beginning in 1944, which used the R-2600-20 Twin Cyclone engine with 1,900hp and Curtiss' four-bladed propeller. The later models also had improved handling, a strengthened

Below: US Marine Corps Curtiss SB2C-4 Helldivers, probably of Marine Scout Bombing Squadron 333 (VMSB-333), pictured at MCAS Ewa, Hawaii.

Above: The Curtiss XSB2C-1 Helldiver prototype (BuNo 1758) during a test flight. The aircraft made its first flight on 18 December 1940 but crashed on 8 February 1941 due to an engine failure during a landing approach. It sustained damage to the fuselage but was repaired. It was later destroyed after suffering an inflight wing failure on 21 December 1941.

Right: Aerial view of an SB2C in the upper landing circle above USS Yorktown in July 1944. Apparent is the deep rear fuselage, the cause of the bad longitudinal stability that would plague the SB2C throughout its service life.

Curtiss SB2C Helldiver

Crew:	Two, pilot and radio operator/gunner
Length:	36ft 8in (11.18m)
Wingspan:	49ft 9in (15.17m)
Height:	13ft 2in (4.01 m)
Empty weight:	10,547lb (4,794kg)
Loaded weight:	16,616lb (7,553kg)
Powerplant:	Wright R-2600-20 Twin Cyclone radial engine of 1,900hp
Top speed:	295mph at 16,700ft (5,090m)
Service ceiling:	29,100ft (8,870m)
Armament:	2× 20mm (0.79in) Mk 2 cannon in the wings, 2× 0.30in (7.62mm) M1919 Browning machine guns in the rear cockpit
Ordnance:	In internal bay: 2,000lb (900kg) of bombs or 1× Mk 13-2 torpedo; on underwing hardpoints: 500lb (225kg) of bombs each

structure and larger tail. Despite its size, the SB2C was much faster than the SBD it replaced. It could keep up with the cruise speed of the fighters. Unlike the SBD, the SB2C also had the added advantage of folding wings. However, one of the faults remaining with the aircraft throughout its operational life was poor longitudinal stability, resulting from a fuselage that was too short due to the necessity of fitting on to aircraft carrier elevators. Although problems persisted throughout its combat service, pilots soon changed their minds about the potency of the Helldiver.

The Helldivers would participate in battles over the Marianas, Philippines (partly responsible for sinking the battleship *Musashi*), Taiwan, Iwo Jima, and Okinawa (in the sinking of the battleship *Yamato*). They were also used

in the 1945 attacks on the Ryuku Islands and the Japanese home island of Honshū in tactical attacks on airfields, communications and shipping. Arguably the nadir of the Helldiver's fortunes occurred during the Battle of the Philippine Sea. Of the 51 SB2Cs that took part in the long-range strike on 20 June 1944, 43 were lost; 15 per cent to Japanese fighters or anti-aircraft fire and 70 per cent to fuel exhaustion or crashes. On the plus side, Helldivers were responsible for more shipping kills than any other aircraft and claimed 44 air-to-air kills, the leading SB2C pilot in this regard being Lt Robert 'Zekie' Parker, later killed by a kamikaze attack.

Despite its shortcomings and the length of time it took to enter service, the SB2C was produced in greater numbers (7,140) than any other dive-bomber in history.

*Above left: **A damaged US Navy SB2C-4E of VB-87 takes the barrier aboard the aircraft carrier USS Ticonderoga (CV-14) during operations off Japan in July-August 1945. Notice that the rear-seat gunner has already begun to make his way out of the cockpit.***

*Above: **Helldiver carrier accidents were not uncommon. Here an SB2C-1 of VB-17 loses its tail during recovery aboard the aircraft carrier USS Bunker Hill (CV-17) during operations in the Caribbean in 1943. The first squadron to receive the Helldiver, VB-17 experienced some growing pains with the type, losing numerous aircraft while operating from shore and aboard the carrier during its shakedown cruise. While flying from Bunker Hill on 11 November 1943, the squadron introduced the Helldiver to combat during a raid on Rabaul.***

*Left: **Crash sequence showing a VB-97 SB2C-4E Helldiver making an approach to the aircraft carrier USS Shangri-La (CV-38) resulting in a ramp strike. Remarkably the pilot, Ens P. Johnson, was unhurt, though his gunner was not so fortunate.***

Above: Plane handlers manoeuvre SB2C-5 of VB-95 into the hangar deck of USS Bunker Hill (CV-17) during operations in the Pacific. Note that the Helldiver only just fits on the elevator, one of the reasons why its fuselage could not be extended to improve its handling.

Right: A US Navy Curtiss SB2C-1C Helldiver of VB-15 landing on the flight deck of the aircraft carrier USS Essex (CV-9) in 1944.

Below: Two Helldivers of VB-83 fly against the backdrop of ships of Task Group 38 operating off Okinawa. VB-83 operated from USS Essex (CV-9), pictured in foreground, during March-September 1945. Note the geometric identification symbols (G-symbols) of the aircraft from the Essex. In the background are the battleship USS Washington (BB-56), a long-hull Essex-class carrier and an Independence-class light carrier.

Left: A SB2C-3 Helldiver of VB-18 'Sunday Punchers' is manoeuvred into position aboard the USS Intrepid (CV-11) after returning from a combat mission during the Battle of Leyte Gulf. The aircraft has suffered battle damage on the tail from Japanese anti-aircraft fire.

Below left: A VB-7 SB2C-3 flies over ships of Task Force 38 after completing an attack against Japanese shipping 40km north of Quinchon, French Indochina, in January 1945. Note the horseshoe symbol on the tail indicating the aircraft's assignment to the USS Hancock and the pillow on the rear cockpit gun in order to provide some level of comfort for the gunner on the long flight home. A Grumman F6F-5 Hellcat from VF-7 is visible in the background.

Bottom left: SB2C-3 of VB-11 flies over a Japanese oiler smoking furiously a few moments after being hit by carrier-based aircraft in the vicinity of French Indochina. VB-11 operated from USS Hornet (CV-12) during October 1944-January 1945, participating in the Battle of Leyte Gulf and flying numerous strikes over the Philippines, Formosa, and Hong Kong. Note the white dot tail symbol indicating the aircraft's assignment to the USS Hornet.

Below: A Japanese Mogami-class cruiser under attack by US Navy aircraft of Carrier Air Group 7 (CVG-7) following the Battle of Leyte Gulf, 26 October 1944. A Curtiss SB2C-3 Helldiver of VB-7 is visible in the upper right of the photograph. The cruiser is most probably Kumano which had her bow blown off by a torpedo launched from the destroyer USS Johnston (DD-557) during the Battle off Samar on 25 October. She was attacked by aircraft of CVG-7 from USS Hancock (CV-19) while retreating through the Sibuyan Sea and was struck by three 500lb (227kg) bombs. She survived and sailed to Manila Bay for repairs on her bow and all four boilers. On 6 November, she was struck by two torpedoes fired from US submarines and finally sunk by aircraft from USS Ticonderoga (CV-14) on 25 November 1944.

Grumman TBF Avenger

The heaviest single-engined aircraft of World War 2, Grumman's eponymous Avenger became one of the most potent torpedo bombers of World War 2. Its design was characterised by its portly fuselage, three-man crew and multi-role capabilities, and it soon began to epitomise the changing tide of war in the Pacific as the US took the battle towards Japan. The success of the Avenger stemmed beyond its use by the US Navy for the aircraft saw extensive service with British and Commonwealth forces as well as becoming a staple of aircraft inventories around the world in the Cold War years.

In 1939, the US Navy's Bureau of Aeronautics issued a request for proposals for a new torpedo/level bomber to replace the outdated Douglas TBD Devastator. For the new aircraft, BuAer specified a crew of three (pilot, bombardier, and radio operator), each armed with a defensive weapon, as well as a dramatic increase in speed over the TBD and an ability to carry a Mark 13 torpedo or 2,000lb of bombs. The US Navy selected a Grumman design as the winner of the competition and placed an order for 286 aircraft on 8 April 1940 – this before its XTBF-1 prototype had even flown. Development proved to be unusually smooth, the only aspect

that proved challenging was meeting a BuAer requirement that called for the rear-facing defensive gun to be mounted in a power turret. Powered by a single Wright R-2600-8 14-cylinder Cyclone radial piston engine, the XTBF-1 made its maiden flight on 1 August 1941 and although it was soon lost in a crash, rapid production continued. During the opening ceremony of Grumman's new production facility intended to manufacture the new XTBF-1, word came down that the Japanese had attacked Pearl Harbor. It has often been stated that this is when the TBF became known as the 'Avenger', but in truth it had been so named months earlier.

Design of the Grumman TBF Avenger was conventional and followed the lessons

Right: **It would never win a beauty contest, but the Grumman TBF Avenger series became one of the most potent torpedo bombers of World War 2. Its rugged construction and legendary ability to absorb punishment endeared it to its aircrews throughout the war.**

Below: **US Navy Avengers aboard USS** Monterey **(CVL-26) preparing for take off for a bombing mission over Tinian Island, the nearest Japanese held island to Saipan in the Marianas in June 1944. The aircraft are from Torpedo Squadron VT-28, Carrier Air Group 28 (CVG-28).**

learned with previous Grumman aircraft attempts including the wide-area wings. There were three crew members: pilot, turret gunner and radioman/bombardier/ventral gunner. One .30in calibre machine gun was mounted in the nose, a .50in (12.7mm) gun was mounted right next to the turret gunner's head in a rear-facing electrically powered turret, and a single .30in hand-fired machine gun mounted ventrally (under the tail), which was used to defend against enemy fighters attacking from below and to the rear. The wings were power-folding and could set flat up against the sides of the fuselage for improved stowage aboard the space-strapped carriers of the day. The undercarriage consisted of two main landing gear legs (retracting under each wing away from the fuselage centreline) and a retractable tail wheel. The undercarriage was reinforced enough that they could double as airbrakes in the dive-bombing role. The Avenger had a large bomb bay, allowing for one Mark 13 torpedo, a single 2,000lb (907kg) bomb, or up to four 500lb (227kg) bombs. Avengers were primarily completed with the Wright R-2600 Cyclone 14-cylinder radial piston engine series outputting 1,700 to 1,900hp with many forms including a supercharger. Top speed was in the vicinity of 275mph with an operational range out to 1,000 miles. The aircraft could hit service ceilings of 30,000ft with a 2,000ft per minute rate-of-climb. The aircraft had overall ruggedness and stability, and pilots say it flew like a truck, which ideally suited its role.

After hundreds of the original TBF-1 models were built, the TBF-1C began production, but by 1943 Grumman began to slowly phase out production of the Avenger to produce F6F Hellcat fighters, and the Eastern Aircraft Division of General Motors took over production, with these aircraft being designated TBM. Starting in mid-1944, the TBM-3 began production (with a more powerful powerplant and wing hardpoints for drop tanks and rockets). The dash 3 was the most numerous of the Avengers (with about 4,600 produced). However, most of the Avengers in service were dash-1s until near the end of the war in 1945.

Initial combat actions for the TBF Avenger were recorded during the famous Battle of Midway on 4 June 1942, but it proved to be a baptism of fire. Of the six aircraft launched into battle with VT-8, only one returned home and this with a wounded bombardier and dead tail gunner. Later in the war, with growing US air superiority, better attack co-ordination and more experienced pilots, Avengers were able to play vital roles in the subsequent battles against Japanese surface forces.

On 24 August 1942, the next major naval battle occurred at the Eastern Solomons. Based on the carriers *Saratoga* and *Enterprise*, the 24 TBFs present were able to sink the Japanese light carrier *Ryūjō* and claim one dive bomber, at the cost of seven aircraft. The first major success for the TBFs was at the battle of Guadalcanal in November 1942, when Marine Corps and Navy Avengers helped sink the battleship *Hiei*, which had already been crippled the night before.

*Below: **The second Grumman XTBF-1 Avenger prototype (BuNo 2540) at the NACA Langley Research Center, in 1942.***

The Royal Navy's Fleet Air Arm also used the Avenger, initially calling the type the TBF Tarpon befoe reverting back to its original name. Beginning in 1943, British squadrons began seeing service in the Pacific as well as

Grumman TBF/TBM Avenger

Crew:	Three: pilot; radioman/ bombardier/ventral gunner; and turret gunner
Length:	40ft 11.5in (12.48m)
Wingspan:	54ft 2in (16.51m)
Height:	15ft 5in (4.7m)
Empty weight:	10,545lb (4,783kg)
Loaded weight:	17,893lb (8,115kg)
Powerplant:	Wright R-2600-20 radial engine of 1,900hp
Top speed:	275mph
Service ceiling:	30,100ft (9,170m)
Armament:	1× 0.30in (7.62mm) nose-mounted M1919 Browning machine gun (on early models) or 2× 0.50in (12.7mm) wing-mounted M2 Browning machine guns; 1× 0.50in (12.7mm) dorsal-mounted M2 Browning machine gun; 1× 0.30 in (7.62mm) ventral-mounted M1919 Browning machine gun
Ordnance:	Up to 2,000lb (907kg) of bombs or 1× 2,000lb (907kg) Mark 13 torpedo
Rockets:	8× 3.5in forward firing aircraft rockets or high velocity aerial rockets

Above: **US Navy TBF-1 Avengers drop their deadly Mark 13 torpedos during a practice sortie. One torpedo could be housed in the bomb bay and the bombardier handled the torpedo responsibility for medium-altitude level attack, but for low-level runs the pilot took over the role using an illuminated sight in the cockpit.**

Below: **The sole survivor of the six VT-8 Grumman Avengers that attacked the Japanese carrier force during the Battle of Midway. Seaman 1st Class Jay D. Manning, who was operating the turret was killed in action with Japanese fighters during the attack. The pilot, Ensign Albert K. Earnest, and the other crewman, Radioman 3rd Class Harry H. Ferrier, both survived the action. The damaged aircraft (TBF-1, BuNo 00380) was photographed near the foot of the Sand Island pier, Midway, on 24 June 1942.**

conducting anti-submarine warfare missions over home waters. The aircraft was also provided to the Royal New Zealand Air Force, which equipped four squadrons with the type during the conflict.

Nicknamed the 'Turkey' by its aircrews because of its size, the Avenger remained the US Navy's primary torpedo bomber for the remainder of the war. While seeing action at key engagements such as the Battles of the Philippine Sea and Leyte Gulf, the Avenger also proved an effective submarine killer. During the course of the war, Avenger squadrons sank around 30 enemy submarines in the Atlantic and Pacific. As the Japanese fleet was reduced later in the war, the TBF/TBM's primary role began to diminish and the Avenger was evolved into a myriad of other useful roles including that of dedicated reconnaissance platform, target towing, airborne early warning (AEW), anti-submarine warfare (ASW) and light carrier-based transport.

Overall, total production of the TBF Avenger series ranged between 9,836 and 9,839 aircraft (sources vary on the exact count).

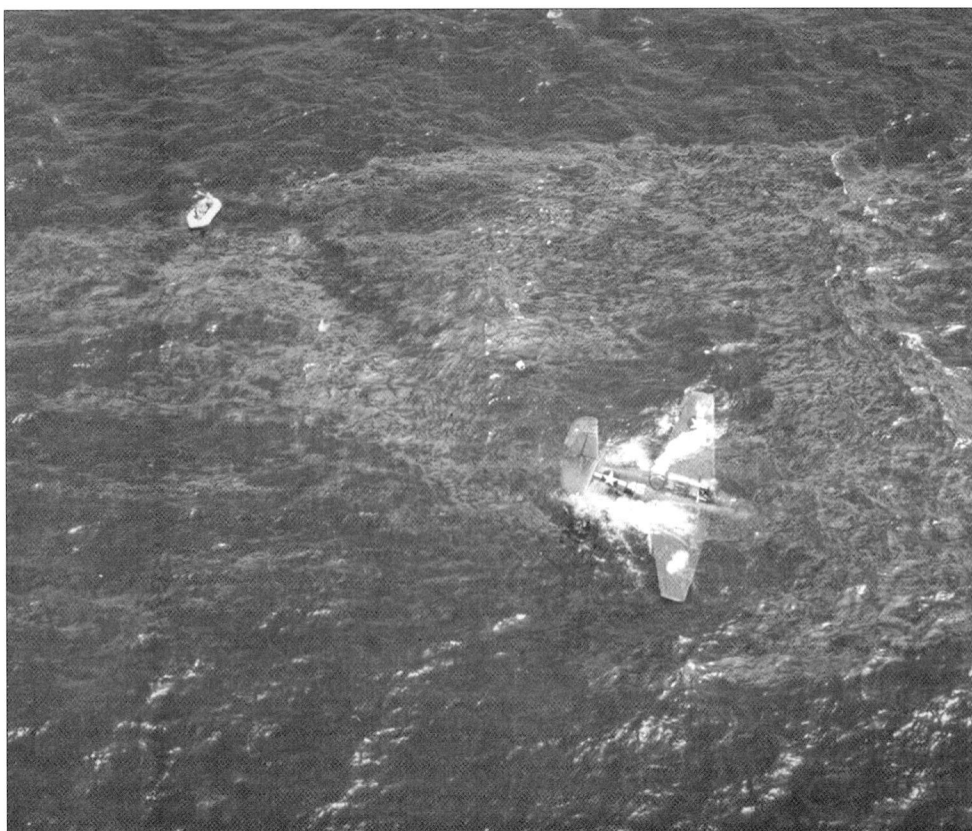

Left: *A US Marine Corps TBM Avenger dropping 227kg bombs over Okinawa. In lieu of a torpedo, the Avenger could stock up to 2,000lb (4x 500lb or 12x 100lb) of conventional bombs for use against surface targets.*

Right: *A deadly Mark 13 torpedo is lowered onto a trolley ready for loading into the open bomb bay of the awaiting Avenger.*

Bottom right: *A US Navy TBM pilot hurrying to his aircraft aboard the USS* Monterey *(CVL-26) for a strike on Guam.*

Bottom left: *The TBF Avenger flown by Ensign Carroll L. Farrell of VT-10 from the aircraft carrier USS* Enterprise *(CV-6), pictured after ditching in the water just outside Truk Lagoon, 30 April 1944. The pilot and his crew are in the raft and were later rescued by the submarine USS* Tang *(SS-306).*

Bottom: *An Avenger of VT-8 is poised for launch from the aircraft carrier USS* Bunker Hill *(CV-17) for a strike against Saipan in June 1944. Note the rocket rails.*

Below: *A TBF-1 about to grab the wire as it touches down on the flightdeck of USS* Intrepid *(CV-11) in 1942.* Intrepid *participated in several campaigns in the Pacific theatre of operations, most notably the Battle of Leyte Gulf.*

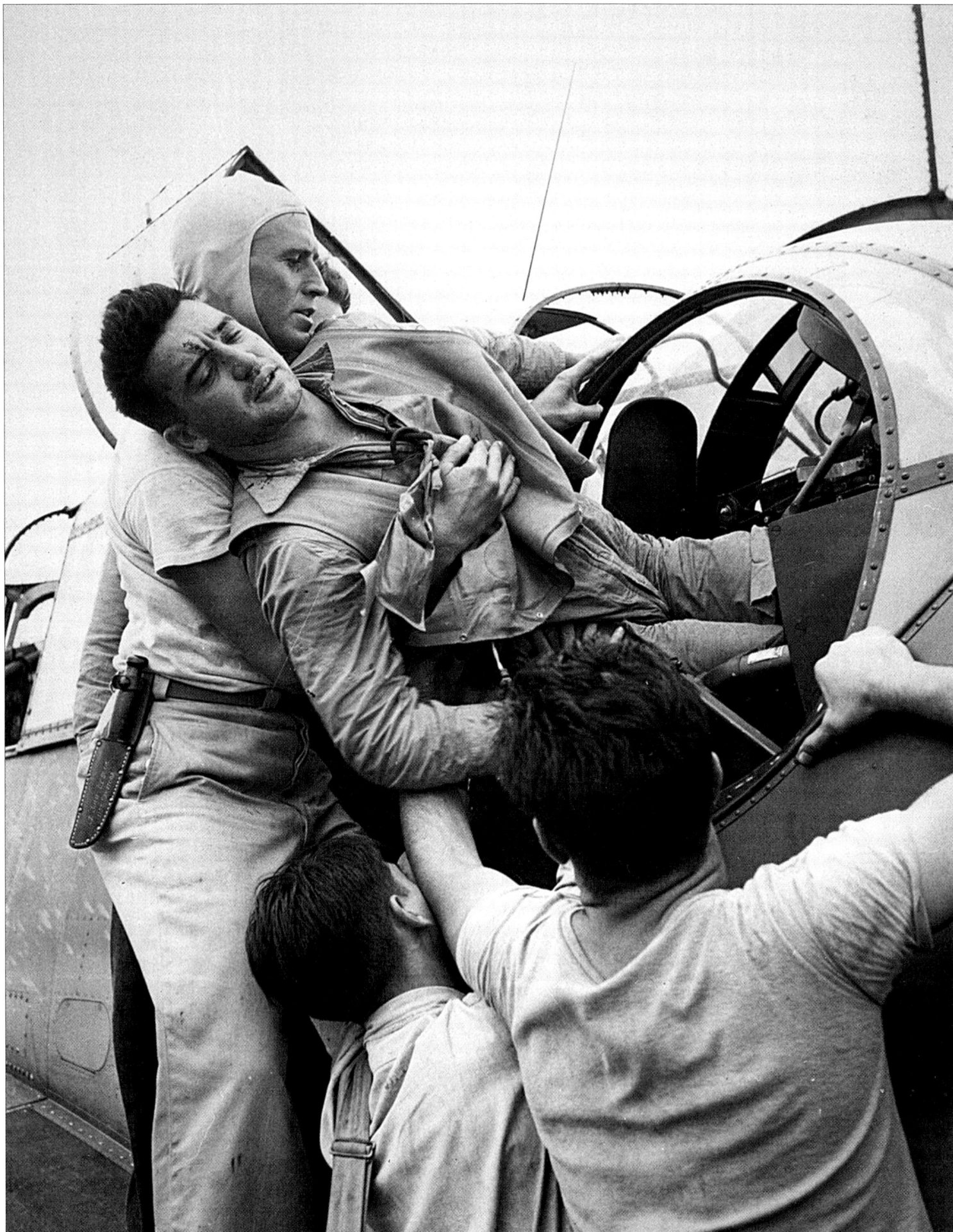

Above: **US Navy TBM Avengers (foreground) and SB2C Helldivers drop bombs on Hakodate in July 1945.**

Left: **Crewmen aboard USS Saratoga lift AOM Kenneth Bratton, USNR, out of a TBF Avenger's rear turret after a raid on Rabaul on 5 November 1943. The aircraft and a friendly F6F Hellcat successfully fought off eight attacking Zeros, downing three. Bratton and pilot Commander Henry Caldwell survived, but sadly the third crewmember, Paul Barnett, was killed in the action.**

Right: **A tractor pulls the battle-damged Grumman TBF-1 Avenger flown by Cliff Largess of VT-10 after it crash landed on the aircraft carrier USS Enterprise (CV-6) having been damaged over Hollandia, New Guinea, in a friendly fire incident with an F6F-3 Hellcat.**

*Right: **US Navy TBF-1 Avenger torpedo bombers flying in echelon formation over Norfolk, VA.***

*Below: **The Avenger was renowned for its ability to absorb a great deal of punishment and still get its crews home, as remarkably illustrated here by this victim of anti-aircraft fire.***

*Above: **Avengers of VT-5 from the USS Yorktown (CV-10) fly over the site where squadron aircraft scored four direct hits on the Japanese destroyer Wakatake, sinking her in just 15 seconds, 110km north of the Palau islands.***

*Below: **Ordnancemen on the flight deck of an unidentified escort carrier, prepare 12.7cm High Velocity Aircraft Rockets (HVAR) and 227kg bombs for loading onto Grumman TBM-3s. The rockets allowed Avenger crews to strike at surface targets with devastating results to the enemy, both physically and psychologically.***

George Bush

In June 1943, future-President George H. W. Bush was commissioned as the youngest naval aviator at the time. Later, while flying a TBM with VT-51 from the USS *San Jacinto* (CVL-30), his TBM was shot down over the Pacific island of Chichi Jima on 2 September 1944. Both of his crewmates were killed, but he was able to release his payload and hit the target before being forced to bail out. For the action he received the Distinguished Flying Cross.

TBF-1C Avenger of VT-51, flown by Lt George Bush, 1944.

Grumman F6F Hellcat

R. G. SMITH

Industrial Aviation
© June, 1945

Left: US Navy Grumman F6F-3 Hellcat of VF-1 on board USS Yorktown in May 1943. Power came from a single Pratt & Whitney R-2800-10 two-row 18-cylinder air-cooled radial engine. It featured two-stage supercharging and water injection to give additional combat power. It drove a three-bladed Hamilton Standard Hydromatic controllable pitch propeller. Cooling was controlled by a ring of moveable gills disposed around the top half of the cowling. The exhaust pipes were clustered in the lower cowling and discharged just above the wing root.

GRUMMAN HELLCAT (F6F-5)

Faster and easier to handle than its predecessor, the F6F-3, the F6F-5 version of the Hellcat has an outstanding performance record in both the Pacific and European areas. Principal external differences between the F6F-5 and the F6F-3 are slightly modified engine cowl flaps and the deep blue overall color of the F6F-5. Powered by a 2000 hp Pratt & Whitney R-2800 engine, the F6F-5 has a top speed of about 380 mph. It has six .50 caliber machine guns, can carry two 1000-lb. bombs and is also equipped to carry rockets. Wing span is 42 ft. 10 in.; length 33 ft. 6⅝ in.; height 14 ft. 5 in.

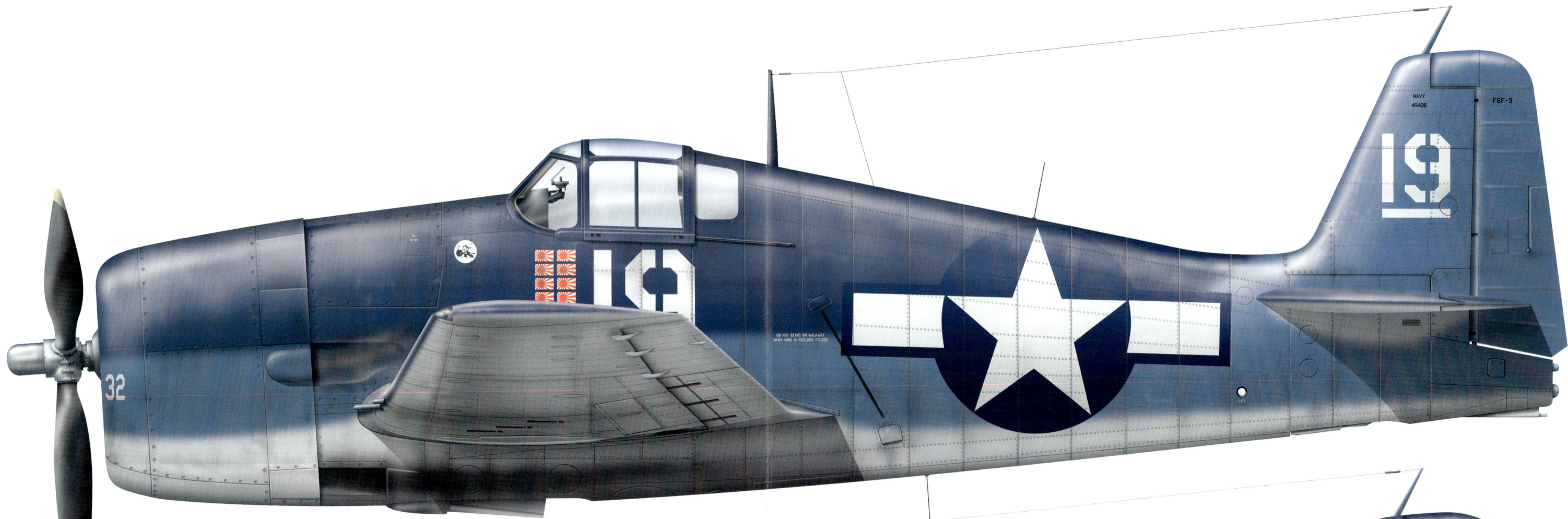

Big, blunt and brutal, the highly effective Grumman F6F Hellcat was one of the few fighter aircraft that could legitimately claim to be a genuine war-winning weapon. It had been designed to incorporate lessons learned in combat, particularly against the Imperial Japanese Navy's agile and deadly Mitsubishi A6M Zero which had come as an unpleasant surprise in December 1941. But the Hellcat's arrival in 1943 signalled the start of a new phase in the Pacific war. The new fighter was equally at home on pitching carrier decks as in the rugged environment of coral airstrips. More importantly, it proved superior to the opposing Japanese fighters, so much so that Hellcats shot down 5,515 enemy aircraft for the loss of 270 in combat. In a front-line career lasting just two years, the F6F became the most prolific American 'ace maker'.

Although the Hellcat incorporated lessons from fighter combat, it was six months before Pearl Harbor, and a whole year before the battle of Midway, when the Grumman Aircraft Engineering Corporation of Bethpage, Long Island, was asked to design a successor to the F4F Wildcat. By that time the Wildcat had only seen action with the Royal Navy, but it was already clear that it was generally outperformed by European contemporaries, never mind the Mitsubishi A6M Navy Type 0, usually known as the Zero, which had yet to be encountered by the Allies.

The XF6-1 from the team headed by Leroy R. Grumman and William T. Schwendler was powered by a Wright R-2600 14-cylinder engine. Grumman was contracted to produce two prototypes, but it soon became apparent that something more powerful was required to counter the Zero. Grumman therefore replaced the R-2600 with the R-2800 Double Wasp which offered 25 per cent more power. Accordingly, the second prototype, designated XF6F-3, was fitted with this engine.

Just five months after the XF6F-3's maiden flight, production aircraft started rolling off the assembly line.

A few minor bugs were eliminated and by the end of 1943 some 2,500 examples had been delivered. Early aircraft had the Pratt & Whitney R-2800-10 engine but later examples featured the more powerful -10W, which featured

Top left: Grumman F6F-3 Hellcat as flown by Lt (jg) Alexander Vraciu of VF-16, US Navy.

Bottom left: Grumman F6F-5 Hellcat as flown by Lt Leo B. McCudden of VF-20, USS Enterprise, October 1944.

water injection. Provision was also made for a 150-gallon drop tank under the fuselage. Nocturnal variants followed. Both the F6F-3E night intruder, of which 18 were produced, and the F6F-3N night fighter (200 built) carried radar antennae in starboard wing pods. The -3E slung its AN/APS-4 unit beneath the wing, while the -5N's AN/APS-6 was faired more smoothly into the wing's lower surface.

Production of the F6F-3 ended in April 1944, by which time it had been replaced by the much improved F6F-5. The Hellcat's basic design was so essentially 'right' that the new version was little more than a product improvement with a re-designed, closer-fitting engine cowling, strengthened airframe, flat windscreen and deleted rear side windows and spring tab ailerons.

The F6F-5 had greater fighter-bomber capability. It could carry additional fuel tanks or two 1,000lb bombs together with racks for six 5in HVARs (high velocity aircraft rockets). There was also an alternate armament arrangement: either the standard six 0.50in-calibre guns or two 20mm cannon and four 0.50in guns. A total of 1,434 F6F-5E/Ns were produced for US Navy and US Marine Corps units and operated from carriers and land bases. Those supplied to the UK were designated Hellcat FRIIs.

From the time of its introduction during a mission against the Japanese-held Marcus Islands on 31 August 1943 until the end of the war, the Hellcat participated in all the US Navy's major actions against the Japanese. By taking a steady toll of enemy aircraft the Grumman fighter made a significant contribution to the

*Above: **An F6F-3 Hellcat near NAS Patuxent River in February 1944. The Hellcat's wing area of 334 sq ft (31 sq m) was bigger than that of any other principal Allied fighter in World War 2 and compares with the Spitfire's 242 sq ft (22.5 sq m) and the Mustang's 233 sq ft (21.6 sq m).***

Allies' victory. But of all the actions involving the Hellcat squadrons, the most spectacular and best remembered – its finest hour, so to speak – came on 19-20 June 1944 during the assault on the Marianas Islands.

In what history calls the Battle of The Philippine Sea, but which the participants came to know as the 'Great Marianas Turkey Shoot', US carrier aircraft inflicted a devastating defeat on the Japanese. The capture of the island chain just 1,400 miles from Japan represented a vital step in the US advance because it made possible the construction of bases from which B-29 bombers could reach Tokyo. Over the whole Marianas campaign, from 11 June to 10 August, the 19 Hellcat squadrons involved claimed to have shot down 869 Japanese aircraft, around 475 of them during the two-day 'Turkey Shoot'.

Hellcats continued to serve with US Navy units but with the F4U Corsair having been cleared for use aboard the fast carriers in 1944, the bent-wing fighter gradually supplemented and then replaced the F6F. US Navy Hellcat squadrons also supported the Allied invasion of southern France in 1945, their only participation in the war in Europe.

Of the total number of 12,272 Hellcats built, incredibly 11,000 of them were manufactured in just two years.

*Left: **Grumman F6F-5 production line at Bethpage in 1944. Grumman earned a reputation for turning out rugged naval aircraft well-suited to the rigours of operating from carrier decks. The Hellcat was no exception. Like its immediate predecessor, the F4F Wildcat, the Hellcat rapidly became known for its ability to absorb battle damage and keep flying. It might not win a beauty contest, but who cared if the aircraft could take it as well as dish it out and get you home safely?***

*Right: **The cockpit was roomy and recognised the need for comfort on long over-water flights. The framed canopy slid backwards to facilitate entry and the aft pair of windows was deleted in the F6F-5. The windscreen was of armoured glass and there was a sheet of armour plating behind the pilot's seat. Vision from the cockpit was improved by the tail-down attitude and the high seating position resulting from the cockpit being located above the fuel tanks.***

*Below: **US Navy aircraft from Carrier Air Group 12 (CVG-12) aboard the USS Saratoga (CV-3) warming up for a strike during the Gilbert Islands campaign. Grumman F6F-3 Hellcats are in the foreground, followed by Grumman TBF-1 Avengers and Douglas SBD-5 Dauntless.***

F6F-3

Engine:	Pratt & Whitney R-2800-10 of 2,000hp
Max speed:	376mph (605km/h) at 17,300ft (5,323m)
Length:	33ft 7in (10.24m)
Wing span:	42ft 10in (12.82m)
Height:	13ft (3.96m)
Armament:	6x 0.50in (12.7mm) machine guns
Max take-off weight:	15,487lb (7,025kg)
Range:	1,085 miles (1,736km)

F6F-5

Engine:	Pratt & Whitney R-2800-10W of 2,000hp
Max speed:	386mph (618km/h)
Length:	33ft 7in (10.24m)
Wing span:	42ft 10in (12.82)
Height:	13ft (3.96m)
Armament:	6x 0.50in (12.7mm) machine guns (alternative: 4x 0.50in machine guns and 2x 20mm cannon)
Max take-off weight:	15,413lb (6,991kg)
Range:	1,040 miles (1,674km) on internal fuel

Above: A formation of F6F-3 Hellcats from VF-1 assigned to Carrier Air Group 1 (CVG-1) aboard the USS Yorktown from May to August 1944. Note the unusual placement of the tactical squadron numbers in large black numbers on the underside of the left wings.

Below: Surrounded by F6F Hellcats, ordnancemen work on bombs in a hangar deck of USS Yorktown, while in the background offficers and men watch a movie. Mounted in a low mid position, the three spar wings of the Hellcat comprised five main assemblies. The centre section passed through the fuselage beneath the cockpit and housed self-sealing fuel tanks. Two stub centre sections provided the attachment points and wheel wells for the main undercarriage units, while the detachable outer panels were arranged to swivel at the front spar and fold aft along the fuselage sides. Ailerons were metal-framed and fabric-covered, and there were split flaps between the ailerons and the fuselage. The wings folded back and pivoted in an ingenious manner for carrier stowage.

Bottom left: US Navy pilots pleased over their victories during the Marshall Islands attack, grin across the tail of a Grumman F6F-3 Hellcat on board the USS Lexington (CV-16), after shooting down 17 out of 20 Japanese aircraft heading for Tarawa in November 1943. The Hellcat achieved a kill: loss ratio of 19:1, higher than any other World War 2 fighter

Above: **A night fighter sub-variant of the Hellcat was the F6F-3N that featured the AN/APS-6 radar in a fairing on the starboard outer wing.**

Above left and left: **Although the Hellcat was a sturdy aircraft and was designed to take the heavy treatment of carrier operations, crashes were not uncommon, as this sequence testifies. Amazingly, the pilot of this Hellcat returning from a mission over the Philippines survived the incident.**

Hellcat Aces

A total of 307 F6F pilots were credited with shooting down five or more enemy aircraft to make them aces and the Hellcat the most successful US fighter ever. Not for nothing was the Hellcat also known as the 'ace maker'.

Hellcat pilots claimed three-quarters of the aerial victories attributed to the US Navy in the Pacific. Navy and Marine F6Fs flew 66,530 combat sorties (45 per cent of the total) of which 62,386 were flown from aircraft carriers. Against its principal adversary, the Mitsubishi Zero, which it had been intended to counter, it achieved a 13:1 kill-to-loss ratio. David McCampbell was the top USN ace, but three other Hellcat pilots scored 20 or more victories against the Japanese.

'I noticed one Zero skirting in and out of clouds and as I made pass at him, he promptly ducked back into them. I played cat and mouse with him for several minutes until I climbed into the sun to let him think I had retreated. When I came down on him for the last time, he never knew what hit him as his wing tanks and cockpit exploded. I ended up splashing four Zeros that day to bring my total aerial victories up to nine kills. Little did I know that within six months I would more than double that score.'

Lt Alex Vraciu (left) recalling one of his victories that made him the US Navy's fourth highest ranking ace.

Above: **An F6F-3 Hellcat from VF-9 flies over the beached Japanese destroyer Tachikaze, during Task Force 58's strikes on the Japanese naval base at Truk, Caroline Islands, 16-17 February 1944. VF-9 was assigned to Carrier Air Group 9 (CVG-9) aboard the USS Essex (CV-9). On 4 February 1944, Tachikaze ran aground at Kuop Atoll in Truk Lagoon while returning from Rabaul, and remained stranded there despite efforts to free her. During the Allied Operation 'Hailstone' on 17–18 February, Tachikaze suffered heavy strafing followed by a torpedo hit in the engine room, which sank the ship by the stern.**

Top right: **Crash landing of F6F-3, Number 30, of VF-2, USS Enterprise, into the carrier's port side 20mm gun gallery on 10 November 1943. Lt Walter L. Chewning, Jr, USNR, the Catapult Officer, is climbing up the Hellcat's side to assist the pilot from the burning aircraft. The pilot, Ensign Byron M. Johnson, escaped without significant injury.**

Right: **An F6F-3 Hellcat from VF-16, Carrier Air Group 16, goes down deck for take-off on the USS Lexington (CV-16) during the Gilbert Islands campaign.**

Douglas BTD-1 Destroyer

The Douglas BTD Destroyer could never be described as a particularly graceful aircraft. Developed to succeed the SBD Dauntless (another Douglas product) and the Curtiss SB2C Helldiver torpedo bomber, owing to the end of the war in August of 1945, total production of BTD Destroyers was limited to just 30 examples, signalling the premature end of the programme.

On 20 June 1941, the US Navy placed an order with the Douglas Aircraft Company for two prototypes of a new two-seat dive bomber to be designated XSB2D-1. The resulting aircraft, designed by a team led by Ed Heinemann, was a purposeful-looking large single-engined mid-winged monoplane. It had a laminar flow gull-wing and, unusually for a carrier-based aircraft of the time, a tricycle undercarriage. It was fitted with a bomb bay and underwing racks for up to 4,200lb (1,900kg), while defensive armament consisted of two wing-mounted 20mm (0.79in) cannon and two remote-controlled turrets, each with two .50in (12.7mm) machine guns.

Designated Douglas XSB2D-1 Destroyer, the first prototype made its maiden flight on 8 April 1943 and it demonstrated strong performance gains over existing types. Such was the promising nature of the design that the US Navy placed a procurement order for 358 aircraft under the SB2D-1 designation. However, before production started the US Navy changed its requirements to a single-seat carrier-based torpedo/dive bomber without defensive turrets. Douglas reworked the SB2D by removing the turrets and second crewman, while adding two wing-mounted 20mm cannon, enlarging the bomb bay and providing increased fuel capacity. Airbrakes were installed in each side of the fuselage and the big Wright Cyclone 18 engine of the XSB2D-1 was retained to give the requisite high performance. The US Navy accepted the revised Destroyer design as the BTD-1 and production began in earnest with first deliveries beginning in June 1944. However, the programme was brought to a crashing

Above: A US Navy Douglas BTD-1 Destroyer (BuNo 04963) in flight near the Naval Air Test Center Patuxent River on 25 July 1944.

Right: A rare shot of the two-seat Douglas XSB2D-1 Destroyer in 1943, sporting two remote-controlled turrets, one dorsal and one ventral (just visible).

Far right: A scale model of the Douglas SB2D Destroyer at the wind tunnel of the Ames Research Center, Moffett Field, CA, on 1 April 1942. Only two XSB2Ds were built plus 28 single seat versions, redesignated BTD-1.

halt when the Japanese Empire surrendered on 15 August 1945. In all, some 30 airframes were completed and delivered, but these were quickly retired from service, never to see combat action against their intended foe in the Pacific.

But all was not lost for Douglas… Heinemann and his team were already working on developing the single-seat BT2D into the Douglas A-1 Skyraider.

Douglas BTD-1 Destroyer

Crew:	One
Length:	38ft 7in (11.76m)
Wingspan:	45ft (13.72m)
Height:	13ft 7in (4.14m)
Empty weight:	11,561lb (5,244 kg)
Loaded weight:	19,000lb (8,618 kg)
Powerplant:	1× Wright R-3350-14 Cyclone 18 radial engine of 2,300hp
Top speed:	334mph at 16,100ft (4,900m)
Service ceiling:	23,600ft (7,195m)
Armament:	2× 20mm AN/M2 (0.79 in) cannons, 200 RPG
Ordnance:	Up to 3,200lb (1,450kg) of bombs in the bomb bay or two 1,947lb torpedoes

Grumman F8F Bearcat

Grumman F8F-1 Bearcat

Crew:	One
Length:	28ft 3in (8.61m)
Wingspan:	35ft 10in (10.92m)
Height:	13ft 9in (4.21m)
Empty weight:	7,070lb (3,207kg)
Loaded weight:	9,600lb (4,354kg)
Powerplant:	1× Pratt & Whitney R-2800-34W Double Wasp two-row radial engine of 2,300hp
Top speed:	42 mph
Service ceiling:	38,700ft (11,796m)
Armament:	4× 0.50in (12.7mm) Browning M2 machine guns
Rockets:	4× 5in (127mm) unguided rockets
Bombs:	1,000lb (454kg) bombs

The last, most powerful of Grumman's prop-driven fighters, the F8F Bearcat has been described as an engine with a saddle on it. Born of experience gained by study of fighter operations from carriers, the F8F was built smaller and lighter than its F6F predecessor, despite being designed around the same big Pratt & Whitney R-2800 engine. The most powerful single-engine aircraft ever built, the F8F out-performed all others in all aspects of combat manoeuvrability

After careful study of air combat operations from carriers, Grumman designed the F8F as a follow-on to its highly successful F6F Hellcat. Given the Grumman designation G-58, work on the Bearcat began in 1943. It was a cantilever, low-wing monoplane of all-metal construction, with the same NACA 230 series wing used in the Hellcat, that folded at about two thirds of the wing span for carrier storage. It

incorporated armour protection for the pilot and had self-sealing fuel tanks installed. It was more than 5ft shorter and 2,000lb lighter, and had a rate of climb 30% higher than its predecessor, the F6F Hellcat. Despite being smaller and lighter, the Bearcat was still powered by the same Pratt & Whitney R-2800 engine used on the F6F and F7F. The Hellcat used a huge four-bladed propeller and keeping the prop clear of the deck required long landing gear, which, combined with the shortened fuselage, gave the Bearcat a significant 'nose-up' profile on land. To minimise drag, a heavier skin was used with flush riveting and spot welding in some areas. Other improvements in aerodynamic design incorporated refinements in the engine cowling, leading edge intakes and a bubble canopy.

Armament consisted of only four Browning M2 .50in guns as this was considered adequate

against the less rugged and less protected Japanese fighters.

The design was completed in November 1943 and an order for two prototypes was placed on 27 November 1943 under the BuAir designation XF8F-1. The first prototype flew on 21 August 1944, only nine months after the design effort started. The initial flight test demonstrated a 4,800ft (1,500m) per minute climb rate and a top speed of 424mph.

By October 1944, the US Navy had ordered 2,023 of the new F8F-1s from Grumman, and an additional 1,876 from the Eastern Aircraft Division of General Motors, the latter designated F3M-1s. Production aircraft

Above: **Pound for pound, the compact Grumman F8F was the most powerful single-engine, propeller-driven aircraft ever built.**

were equipped with the P&W R-2800-34W engine and boasted a slight increase in fuel capacity. Deliveries began in May 1945 with the first aircraft going to Fighting Squadron VF-19. V-J Day brought cancellation of the GM contract, however, and reduced the buy from Grumman to 770 aircraft.

In many ways, the Grumman F8F Bearcat was the pinnacle of US piston-engine fighter design. The aircraft arrived within the waning months of World War 2, missing combat action in all theatres, but still managed to leave a legacy of power and performance even with the advent of the jet age.

X-Planes and other aircraft: 1941-45

The following is a selection of US carrier aircraft that either failed to pass the prototype testing stage and achieve production, or entered production too late to see active service in World War 2. Once again, they are ordered under the dates of their maiden flights. It is noteworthy that the final entry is the McDonnell XFD-1 Phantom, the first all-jet fighter for the US Navy; thus, the US entered the war in December 1941 with biplane fighters still operating off carriers and ended it less than four years later with its first jet fighter being readied for operations. In the process, speed and climb performance of its aircraft had more than doubled, such was the technological pace of progress driven by war.

GRUMMAN XF5F-1 SKYROCKET

In 1938 Grumman presented a proposal to the US Navy for a twin-engine carrier-based aircraft quite unlike any other fighter aircraft before. Designated the XF5F-1, the design was for a light weight fighter (under 10,000lb maximum take-off weight) powered by two 1,200hp Wright R-1820 engines, with propellers geared to rotate in opposite directions to cancel out the effects of each engine's torque, promising high-speed and an outstanding rate of climb. But what grabbed attention was its peculiar configuration that saw the wing extend beyond the fuselage nose. The Skyrocket flew for the first time on 1 April 1940 and modifications quickly followed the test flights, that included reducing the height of the cockpit canopy, revising the armament installation to four 0.5in (12.7mm) machine guns in place of the cannon, redesign of the engine nacelles, adding spinners to the propellers, and (bowing to conventional aerodynamics) extending the fuselage forward of the wing. These changes were completed on 15 July 1941. The flying qualities were good overall with excellent climbing performance, but by then the US Navy had decided on the Wildcat for mass production and Grumman decided to turn its attention to developing the more-advanced XF7F-1 (Tigercat) and used the XF5F-1 to support the development of the newer design. The prototype continued to be used in various tests, although plagued by various landing gear problems, until it was struck from the list of active aircraft after it made a belly landing on 11 December 1944.

BELL XFL-1 AIRABONITA

The US Navy placed a contract with the Bell Aircraft Corporation on 8 November 1938 for a single prototype of a modified version of the company's XP-39 Airacobra fighter that was currently under development. The chief difference between the two was the adoption of a tailwheel configuration compared to the tricycle gear of the land-based version. The XFL-1 was powered by a single Allison XV-1710-6 piston engine installed amidships behind the pilot and driving a three-bladed Curtiss propeller in the nose via a 10.38ft (3.16m) extension shaft. The aircraft had provisions for a single 37mm (1.46in) Oldsmobile T9 cannon, which could be replaced by a .50in (12.7mm) Browning M2/AN machine gun through the propeller shaft and two .30in (7.62mm) machine guns in the fuselage nose. The Allison engine was the first of its type to be tried out by the Navy and lacked the turbosupercharger fitted to the XP-39. Although the aircraft first flew on 13 May 1940, problems with the Allison engine delayed delivery of the Airabonita to the US Navy until February 1941 and then undercarriage troubles caused the aircraft to fail its carrier qualification trials. By late 1941, the XFL-1 was back with Bell for further modifications, but US Navy interest in the type waned quickly after the start of the war and further development was cancelled.

BREWSTER SB2A BUCCANEER

The Brewster SB2A Buccaneer was a scout/bomber built for the US Navy during the early 1940s. A development of Brewster's earlier SBA scout-bomber, it was larger, had a more powerful engine and could carry up to 1,000lb (454kg) of bombs in an internal bomb bay. For defensive purposes it was fitted with a power-operated turret armed with two .30in machine guns supplementing a further four forward-firing guns. The US Navy ordered a prototype XSB2A on 4 April 1939, which first flew on 17 June 1941. However, large-scale orders had already been placed by this time, with the UK ordering 750 aircraft as the Brewster Bermuda and the Netherlands ordering a further 162. The first US Navy production order, for 140 aircraft, was placed on 24 December 1940, but despite its relatively high pre-war production numbers, the Buccaneer was another light bomber design that was more or less made obsolete by the fast-paced nature of the war. Most were never used in active combat.

CONSOLIDATED TBY-2 SEA WOLF

The Consolidated TBY-2 Sea Wolf was the production version of the XTBU-1 torpedo bomber developed by Vought at the same time as the Grumman Avenger. The XTBU-1 was very similar to the Avenger, although with a less 'chunky' appearance. The first prototype flew on 22 December 1941 and was delivered to NAS Anacostia in March 1942. This placed it several months behind the Avenger, which had made its maiden flight in August 1941. Although the XTBU-1 was 30mph faster than the Grumman design, it suffered from several disadvantages. The first was that the Avenger was already in production by the time the prototype XTBU-1 reached Anacostia. With their wings folded the XTBU-1 took up more space than the Avenger, reducing the number that could be carried on each carrier. Finally Vought's own production facilities were fully occupied building F4U Corsairs. The US Navy sat on the XTBU-1 for well over a year, before deciding to put it into production after all. In September 1943 Consolidated Vultee received an order to build 1,100 of the redesignated TBY-2 Sea Wolf at their new factory at Allenstown, PA. The production TBYs were radar-equipped, with a radome under the right-hand wing. The first aircraft flew on 20 August 1944, but by this time the Avenger equipped every torpedo squadron in the US Navy. Surplus to requirements, Sea Wolf production was cancelled and the 180 already built were used for training missions.

GRUMMAN F7F TIGERCAT

Ordered by the US Navy in June 1941, the XF7F-1 was Grumman's second attempt at a twin-engine fighter, the first having been the unsuccessful XF5F-1 Skyrocket. The new fighter, intended for use aboard the large Midway-class carriers, would be the first carrier aircraft to employ tricycle landing gear. The new aircraft, while designated a fighter, was heavily armed to perform as a ground support aircraft, equipped with four 20mm cannon and four .50in machine guns. It also was capable of carrying two 1,000lb bombs on underwing stations or one torpedo under the fuselage. First flown in December 1943, the XF7F-1 was hurried into production to meet US Marine Corps demands for 500 of the aircraft to support Pacific operations. Deliveries began in April 1944, but changes in operational requirements led to production delays. With 34 single-seat models delivered, production switched to a two-seat night fighter, designated the F7F-2N, a total of 65 of which were built. Grumman then built 189 F7F-3s, which were similar to the F7F-1, but modified with higher rated Pratt & Whitney R-2800-34W engines. Further production under the original contract was cancelled as war's end drew near, but a separate contract produced 60 more F7F-3Ns and 13 F7F-4Ns, production ending in late 1946. The first USMC unit to convert to the Tigercat was VMF(N)-533 which arrived in Okinawa with its F7F-2Ns on 14 August 1945, the day before the Japanese surrender. Too late for service in World War 2, the Tigercat later performed close air support, night fighter, reconnaissance and utility missions during the Korean War. Well designed, the F7F was one of the fastest fighters of the World War 2 era. Unfortunately, its operational life coincided with the advent of more powerful, faster jet aircraft, rendering it obsolete after only a few short years.

RYAN FR-1 FIREBALL

The Ryan FR-1 Fireball fighter was something of a unique creation in the annals of US Navy aviation. The fighter fielded two individual powerplants – a radial piston engine and a turbojet engine – within a single airframe. Design of the FR-1 began in 1943 for a mixed-powered fighter because early jet engines had sluggish acceleration and were considered unsafe and unsuitable for carrier operations. The XFR-1 was a single-seat, low-wing monoplane with tricycle landing gear. A Wright R-1820-72W Cyclone radial engine was mounted in the fighter's nose while a General Electric I-16 (later redesignated as the J-31) turbojet was mounted in the rear fuselage. The revolutionary XFR-1 was also the first US carrier aircraft to feature laminar flow airfoil. The Fireball was lightly armed with four .50in (12.7mm) M2 Browning machine guns mounted in the centre section of the wing. Four 5in (127mm) rockets could be carried under each outer wing panel and two hardpoints were provided under the centre section. Ryan received a contract for three XFR-1 prototypes, the first of which made its maiden flight on 25 June 1944. All three were lost in crashes but

Ryan received orders for 100 production FR-1s, with a follow-up order of 1,000 additional fighters in January 1945. However, only 66 aircraft were built before Japan surrendered in August 1945. Unfortunately for Ryan, the Fireball arrived simply too late to see combat action in World War 2 and subsequently fell out of favour with the post-war US military looking for 'all-jet' systems. Fireball production lasted for just one year and its life span covered two short years before it was retired in favour of more potent and modern systems.

CURTISS XF14C

In 1941, the US Navy issued a requirement for a well-armed, carrier-borne monoplane interceptor featuring a new high performance Lycoming XH-2470-4 series liquid-cooled inline piston engine, a departure from its usual preference for air-cooled engines. Curtiss-Wright was awarded a development contract on 30 June 1941 for two complete prototypes under the designation of XF14C. Early in the development the US Navy requested better altitude performance and, in view of unsatisfactory progress in the development of the XH-2470 engine, Curtiss adapted the design of the aircraft around the new turbocharged Wright R-3350 Duplex-Cyclone air-cooled radial engine and three bladed contra-rotating propellers, designated the XF14C-2. The XF14C-1 was formally cancelled in December of 1943 which allowed focus on the XF14C-2 design which flew for the first time in July 1944. However, performance of the type was still lacking when compared to its contemporaries and exceptional vibrations of the aircraft in flight were noted during testing. Additionally, the XR-3350 series engine consistently demonstrated teething issues that proved it unsuitable for the short term. Coupled with the evaporating tactical need for an extremely high-altitude fighter, the programme was cancelled.

DOUGLAS AM MAULER

Like the Douglas AD Skyraider, the AM Mauler was designed to meet a US Navy requirement combining the bombing and torpedo missions into one aircraft. The aircraft began life when Martin's Model 210 design proposal gained a contract for two XBTM-1 prototypes, the first being flown initially on 26 August 1944. The XBTM-1 was a low-winged, all-metal monoplane with folding wings to allow more compact storage in carrier hangar decks. Its fuselage was an oval-shaped stressed-skin semi-monocoque with the single-seat cockpit and its teardrop-shaped canopy positioned just aft of the air-cooled engine. The large wing consisted of a two-spar centre section with hydraulically-folded three-spar outer panels. The fixed armament of four 20mm (0.79in) T-31 autocannon was fitted in the centre section adjacent to the outer wing panels with 200 rounds per gun. Numerous underwing hardpoints allowed the aircraft to carry an incredible payload. The first XBTM-1 made its maiden flight on 26 August 1944 and began flight testing after it reached the Naval Air Test Center (NATC) on 11 December. The Navy ordered 750 more aircraft on 15 January 1945 although this was reduced to 99 after the surrender of Japan in August. Only 149 AM-1s (excluding prototypes) were completed when production finally ended in October 1949. Initial deliveries to an active unit went to VA-17A on 1 March 1948, but these aircraft saw little front-line service.

BOEING XF8B

The Boeing XF8B was a multi-purpose fighter and attack aircraft developed in response to a US Navy specification issued in 1943. It was far more advanced than the previous generation of Boeing fighter aircraft, which had appeared in the mid 1930s. The XF8B-1 (Boeing Model 400) was designed to serve as a fighter, interceptor, long range escort fighter, fighter-bomber and torpedo-bomber. Boeing was duly awarded a contract to produce three prototypes. It was powered by a four-row Pratt & Whitney XR-4360-10 radial engine, driving a six-bladed contra-rotating propeller. The low mounted wings were straight edged but tapered. The cockpit was mounted above the rear half of the wing. The XF8B could carry six wing mounted guns, either 0.5in machine guns or 20mm cannon. It had an internal bomb bay capable of carrying two 1,600lb bombs and could carry another 3,200lb of bombs externally. The XF8B was the heaviest carrier-based aircraft to be produced during World War 2. The first prototype made its maiden flight on 27 November 1944 and although the XF8B-1 was an impressive aircraft it appeared too late in the conflict to be considered for production. The last two prototypes were completed after the war, but despite its formidable capabilities, the XF8B-1 was fated to never enter series production.

CURTISS XF15C

The aircraft that, in the event, proved to be the last Curtiss US Navy fighter, had its genesis in the service's interest in composite-powered machines. The XF15C was to use a 2,700lb thrust de Havilland H1-B Goblin turbojet, produced in the US by Allis-Chambers. The turbojet was mounted just behind the wing, with the exhaust pipe in the middle of the rear fuselage, eliminating the long tail pipe used on other jets. A 2,100hp Pratt & Whitney air-cooled radial engine was mounted in the nose. The Navy was interested in the Curtiss design, and ordered three prototypes on 7 April 1944. The basic outline of the XF15C was similar to standard piston-engined fighters of that period. It had low-mounted tapered wings, with the pilot sitting just above the leading edge. As first built it had a low set horizontal tail, so only the jet exhaust pipe and the associated kink in the tail singled it out. The first prototype was completed without the jet engine and made its maiden flight on 27 February 1945. The jet was then installed, but the aircraft was lost when it crashed during a landing approach on 8 May 1945. The second prototype made its maiden flight on 8 July 1945 and the third followed soon afterwards. Shortly after this they were given 'T' tails, with the horizontal surfaces mounted at the top of the tail. This configuration was novel at the time but came into use towards the end of the 1950s. The XF15C could reach 469mph at 25,000ft with both engines in use, a significant improvement on the Ryan FR-1 Fireball. However the XF15C wasn't delivered to the Navy until November 1946, by which time jet engines had improved to the point where the Navy was no longer interested in composite construction and instead wanted pure jet aircraft.

DOUGLAS XTB2D SKYPIRATE

The Douglas TB2D Skypirate was a torpedo bomber intended for service with the US Navy's Midway- and Essex-class aircraft carriers; it was too large for earlier decks. Its origins began in 1942 when Douglas designers Ed Heinemann and Bob Donovan began work on a new project to replace the TBD Devastator torpedo bomber, named the Devastator II. On 31 October 1943, just four days after the new Midway class aircraft carriers were ordered into production, Douglas received a contract for two prototypes, designated TB2D, receiving the official name Skypirate. The TB2D was powered by a Pratt & Whitney XR-4360-8 supercharged radial piston engine of 3,000hp driving a pair of four-bladed contra-rotating propellers. An internal bomb bay was part of the original design plans as well, while a rear turret would be used to defend against trailing aerial threats. A rather modern tricycle undercarriage was fitted to allow the large blades the necessary clearance while also simplifying ordnance loading/reloading. A three-man crew would operate the various on-board systems and their stations were fully armoured for low-altitude combat flying. The wings folded outboard of the main landing gear legs for optimal carrier storage and each held two hardpoints for carrying 2,100lb torpedo loads (or conventional drop ordnance equivalent). Each wing was also outfitted with 2x 0.50in Browning M2 heavy machine guns for forward strafing of ground targets. Two prototypes were completed and after many delays a Skypirate prototype finally made it airborne on 13 March 1945, albeit without its dorsal turret. However, the dedicated torpedo bomber was becoming an outdated concept, and with the end of World War 2, the type was deemed unnecessary and cancelled.

MCDONNELL XFD-1 PHANTOM

On New Year's Eve 1942, the US Navy Bureau of Aeronautics called James S. McDonnell, founder of McDonnell Aircraft Corp, offering the company a contract to design and build the first US jet fighter capable of taking off from and landing on an aircraft carrier. Westinghouse Electric Corporation was commissioned to design the turbojet engines, and together the teams took on the challenge. After exhaustive tests on the number and size of the jet engines, it was determined that two 19in-diameter turbojets mounted in the wing roots would provide the necessary power and fuel economy. The final configuration emerged with two Westinghouse 19 XB-2B engines, a low-wing, single-tail fuselage with the horizontal stabiliser clear of the exhaust, and a single cockpit forward of the leading edge of the wing. The nose held four 0.50in guns. When the first XFD-1 was completed in January 1945, only one Westinghouse 19XB-2B engine was available for installation. Ground runs and taxi tests were conducted with the single engine, and such was the confidence in the aircraft that the first flight on 26 January 1945 was made with just the one turbojet engine.

During flight tests, the Phantom became the first naval aircraft to exceed 500mph. With successful completion of tests, a production contract was awarded on 7 March 1945 for 100 FD-1 aircraft. With the end of the war, the Phantom production contract was reduced to 30 aircraft, but was soon increased back to 60. The first prototype was lost in a fatal crash on 1 November 1945, but the second and final Phantom prototype was completed early the next year and became the first purely jet-powered aircraft to operate from an American aircraft carrier, completing four successful take-offs and landings on 21 July 1946, from USS *Franklin D. Roosevelt*.

SUBSCRIBE

TO *YOUR* FAVOURITE MAGAZINE

AND SAVE

Aeroplane traces its lineage back to the weekly The Aeroplane launched in June 1911, and is still continuing to provide the best aviation coverage around. Aeroplane magazine is dedicated to offering the most in-depth and entertaining read on all historical aircraft.

www.aeroplanemonthly.com